PHOTOGRAPHY SPEAKS

66 Photographers on Their Art

PHOTOGRAPHY SPEAKS

66 Photographers on Their Art

Brooks Johnson

Aperture/The Chrysler Museum

Hardcover ISBN: 0-89381-354-0

Paperback ISBN: 0-89381-355-9

Library of Congress Catalog Number: 89-84129

Designed by Germaine Clair

Typeset by B.F. Martin, Inc.

Printed by Teagle and Little, Inc.

Printed and bound in the United States of America

TR
650
.P479
1989

Aperture Foundation, Inc., publishes a periodical, books, and portfolios of fine photography to communicate with serious photographers and creative people everywhere. A complete catalog is available upon request. Address: 20 East 23 Street, New York, NY 10010.

CONTENTS

Preface   vi

Acknowledgements   vii

Introduction   1

Photography Speaks   5

Bibliography   139

Index   141

Preface

Yes, this is a book about photographs. But it is also a book about love, passion, obsession and respect. First it is about the passion of people who make photographs. It is also about the love and obsession that people who collect these photographs have for the medium. Lastly, it is about my own respect for the ultimate medium of art and communication in the twentieth century.

This book began as an accompaniment to the inaugural exhibition of the Chrysler Museum's Alice and Sol B. Frank Photography Gallery, which replaced the museum's nine-year-old photography gallery in 1987. The inaugural exhibitions for both old and new galleries were drawn from a private collection I first encountered in the summer of 1978. As a young photographer for the Chrysler, I had gone with the museum's Chief Curator and the head of our local photography support group to select the opening exhibition. I vividly recall spending all day viewing the photographs. For someone only two years out of art school seeing a myriad of master photographs in one home was a revelatory experience.

Nine years later the collectors were again asked to loan their photographs. In discussions with them I attempted to gain some insight into their collecting interests. I wanted to find out what made this assemblage of photographs different from other collections. The first images they acquired nearly twenty years ago were architectural views. Since then the collection has expanded tremendously and now encompasses all forms of the art. The simple truth, I realized, was that they had acquired what they felt they would enjoy living with. Their love of photography is evident by the number of photographs on the walls of their apartment; a cursory count reveals at least seventy. With over 1,000 more in cabinets, these are people who clearly love and are obsessed with the photographic medium. Photography has brought them a great deal of pleasure over the years; additionally, it has opened their eyes to an exciting way of seeing the world.

This book is not intended to be another picture book on the history of photography or on one family's collection. The straightforward concept of publishing the photographers' statements on their own work can also be found in several other books. However, this book includes the reproduction of a photograph along with biographical information placing the artist within an historical context.

From the living artists I requested a statement on working methods or philosophy. The responses were quite varied. One photographer refused to make a statement and did not want anything printed stating that a text was refused. This person did, however, generously grant permission to reproduce the photograph. After a little coaxing (or even a little arm twisting) a statement was finally received. Some artists sent previously written statements while others wrote something specfically for this book. Most of the deceased artists' statements were obtained from previously published materials.

The photograph-statement-biography format is intended to fill an educational need not currently being met. It is the collectors' and my hope that it will provide the uninitiated with an enjoyable, yet meaningful, introduction to the history of photography. The assemblage of images found in this book indicates what photography means to the collectors. The artists' statements reveal what photography represents to the practitioners. And from this book it is hoped that the reader *and the viewer* will obtain a better understanding of why this medium occupies such a vital and important place in our society.

Acknowledgements

Thanks are due to the many people who have assisted in this project. It begins with thanks to the photographers for not only making the images, but for allowing them to be reproduced in this anthology. Thanks also to the photographers' estate representatives, assistants and gallery and museum personnel who have facilitated my requests. These people include: Hattula Moholy-Nagy, Noya Brandt, Edna Bullock, Kevin E. Smith, Gerd Sander, Wilma Wilcox, Sonja Bullaty, John Lawrence, Howard Chapnick, Anthony Montoya, Sara F. Stevenson, Thomas W. Southall, Paula Stewart, Peter Bunnell, Terence Pitts, Edwynn Houk, Peter MacGill and Laurence Miller.

Thanks to the people who have provided counsel and assistance in various capacities: John Szarkowski, Beaumont Newhall, Phillip S. Block, Jeffrey Hoone and especially William A. Ewing. Warmest thanks to Joyce F. and Robert B. Menschel for their genial support and inspiration.

Thanks also to the Chrysler Museum staff, especially: Roger Clisby, Catherine Jordan, Irene Roughton, Jefferson Harrison, Georgia Lasko, Scott Wolff, Willis Potter, Bernie Jacobs, Jim Armbruster, Patricia Sisk, Stephanie Bagley, Lynda Wright, Rena Hudgins, Robin Maurice and former museum staff David W. Steadman and Amy Ciccone.

Thanks to all of the Aperture staff, especially Michael Hoffman and Steve Dietz. Thanks to George Slade for his assistance with the biographical statements and essay. For the book production thanks to Elawna Sisley and Deborah Marquardt. Special thanks to Germaine Clair for her splendid design and for doing all of the countless tasks necessary to make this collection of photographs and texts into a book.

A final thanks to Mrs. Sol B. Frank, also known as Alice.

Introduction

It must not be forgotten that water-colour drawing and etching have both been despised in their time by artists, dealers, and the public, but they have lived to conquer for themselves places of honour. The promising boy, photography, is but fifty years old. What prophet will venture to cast his horoscope for the year 2000?

Peter Henry Emerson, 1889[1]

This book presents a particular history of photography, one realized through the commingling of words and images from individuals uniquely qualified to offer insight — the practitioners themselves, the artists who give photography a voice. Within a century-and-a-half, photography has dramatically transcended the bounds of traditional creative media; nearly fifty billion photographs are now made annually, with an influence so pervasive and immense that it has surpassed being described as unwieldy. Naturally, most of those fifty billion are personal snapshots of events such as birthday parties or summer vacations and those intended for commercial use, but a significant number of photographs have been and are being made with artistic intent. A survey of photography is impossible to assess completely in any single volume. The enormous 1988 edition of *Contemporary Photographers* contains over 700 entries, and there are surely dozens upon dozens more who might have been included. Given the impossibility of incorporating every artist's work, histories of the medium are necessarily selective; this one is no exception and its parameters may be more closely defined than most.

Since the inception of the medium in 1839, people have collected photography. The first collections consisted of images of friends, relatives and foreign lands. During an age when travel was considerably more arduous than it is today, photographs of unusual locales and the so-called wonders of the world were highly prized; though journeys to the Sphinx, the Parthenon or the Yosemite Valley were dangerous and impractical, one could possess views of these exotica through the surrogate presence of photography. Even now, when travel has been made considerably easier and very few spots on the globe remain unvisited or undocumented, millions of collections exist which consist primarily of images of family and friends in exotic or everyday locations.

The photographs assembled for this book distinguish themselves from the mainstream on several levels; they are the product of that small fraction of photographic activity which involves the artistic intent of individuals working over a period of time and they are drawn from the collection of another individual, unrelated to the photographers, who has selected images based entirely on their *intrinsic value as works of art*. This type of collecting, involving different artists and styles, is a relatively recent activity and, it is probably fair to say, there are proportionally as few collectors out of the whole operating in this mode as there are photographers creating images to interest them.

The reasons why people engage in the photographic art are as varied as the people themselves and the types of images that they make. Recording the observations of these individuals about their medium seemed to be a worthwhile pursuit since photography, to use an oft-applied adjective, is mute. There are, however, different avenues of thought over the usefulness of having an artist speak about his or her work. There are those who believe that the work of art should stand alone, without the encumbrance of further comment by the artist, even without consideration of the historical context within which the artist lived. Some believe, as did T.S. Eliot, that such things as correspondence, drafts and journals are not to be considered in evaluating the artist's work. If an artist's chosen medium is visual, isn't it somewhat irrational to expect him or her to express thoughts or feelings in words? Conversely, however, who is better qualified than the creator of an artwork to elucidate the artist's intentions, issues and motivations?

Communicating such aspects of one's work in writing is frequently considered difficult, perhaps even more so for an artist whose foremost means of expression is visual. Wynn Bullock's comment on the crossover is enlightening:

> Writing is a very painful activity and I'm not good at it in terms of producing an elegant result. I have reams of the most awful notes to testify to that. The process itself, however, is extremely useful to me for it helps to clarify my thinking. And, very occasionally, I do actually arrive at what I want to say in the way I want to say it. When I do, I am thrilled and feel it was worth all the agonizing effort.[2]

What Bullock declines to mention, as do most photographers who complain about the difficulty of writing, is that photography is etymologically identified as writing, though with light as the instrument rather than pen or pencil. Actually, the term "light writing" is somewhat of a misnomer. Light is crucial to the process, of course. But the activity of photographing is more closely linked to editing than writing; the subject — the physical world around us — already exists and the photographer is responsible for coalescing scenes drawn from it, from the already written text of physical facts.

What is remarkable about photography is the medium's ability to function in such a multitude of ways and to reassemble reality in such diverse guises. Perhaps even more intriguing is its ability to act simultaneously in various capacities. Included within what we call fine art photography are the traditions of abstract, social documentary or humanistic, narrative, surrealistic, geometric or design-oriented and conceptual image-making, none of which entirely excludes any other. Photography's frightening ability to be used for political purposes or propaganda reminds us that there is no single, absolute meaning to a given image. Photographic truth is malleable; both the image-maker and the image-user are in possession of a medium that can significantly alter the way we perceive the world and process the information it contains.

It is an essential characteristic of photography that its artistic statements are still records of facts; the grammar of photography is confined to nouns. This can be found in the work of Aaron Siskind, a pioneer in purely abstract imagemaking who began his photographic career as an urban documentarian. His later photographs function much like abstract paintings; he has admitted to influences from the abstract expressionist movement in painting. Although all photographs are documentary by nature they are also abstractions in that they transform the three-dimensional, unconstrained, multi-hued world we experience into two-dimensional, bordered fields, often monochrome in appearance. Siskind's *New York 1,* included in this book, is an abstract image. However, it is at the same time a document of the fact of a broken window.

In the nineteenth century, some individuals earned a living using photography in its strictly factual application, and seem to have accepted the limitations of direct transcription. Eugène Atget placed a sign outside of his domicile stating, "Documents for Artists," making his images available as references to those who either could not or would not transport themselves to sites around Paris. Although these photographers claimed to be making straightforward documents, intimations of artistic intent are inescapable. The care with which they assembled their compositions is evident when we begin to look at and study the images. Many of these early photographers were painters before they took up the new invention. Charles Baudelaire, in his review of "The Salon of 1859," chastised these individuals as well as the new medium itself:

> . . . the photographic industry was the refuge of every would-be painter, every painter too ill-endowed or too lazy to complete his studies, this universal infatuation bore not only the mark of a blindness, an imbecility, but had also the air of a vengeance. I do not believe, or at least I do not wish to believe, in the absolute success of such a brutish conspiracy, in which, as in all others, one finds both fools and knaves; but I am convinced that the ill-applied developments of photography, like all other purely material developments of progress, have contributed much to the impoverishment of the French artistic genius, which is already so scarce.[3]

Some of today's most collected photographers worked in other media before becoming successful with photography. No one would accuse them of being lazy or ill-endowed. Rather, they are employing a tool that more eloquently expresses their ideas. Photography allows them to voice issues they never could with painting or sculpture. It is interesting to note that upon the invention of photography most photographers were primarily concerned with obtaining a technically good image. But as their familiarity with the mechanics of the medium grew, they were able to transform technical proficiency into expressive fluency and to create images motivated by artistic intent. As P.H. Emerson noted, "the painter learns his technique in order to speak," and reminded his audience that "the point is what you have to say, and how to say it." The debate between form and content (how versus what), an essential dialectic of photographic art, continues to this day. Interestingly, the discussion has proceeded to the point where many contemporary photographers are less concerned with image quality than with the idea represented by the photograph.

Despite Baudelaire's misgivings, photography has not caused the decline of artistic genius. Instead, human creativity has been stretched in ways that could never have been imagined. Other media have been propelled forward by the accomplishments of photography. Picasso commented to Brassaï, the painter turned photographer:

Why should the artist persist in treating subjects that can be established so clearly with the lens of a camera? It would be absurd, wouldn't it? Photography has arrived at a point where it is capable of liberating painting from all literature, from the anecdote, and even from the subject. In any case, a certain aspect of the subject now belongs in the domain of photography. So shouldn't painters profit from their newly acquired liberty and make use of it to do other things?[4]

The invention of photography is now 150 years old. This wondrous medium has become an integral part of our world. It influences our lives numerous times on any given day. It is hard to imagine contemporary life without photographs. The statements in this book, extracted from photographers who represent the spectrum of photographic activity and whose comments are as varied in their articulation as are their images, provide testimony to the creative intelligences that have formed the medium as we know it. Even P.H. Emerson in his most optimistic moment would undoubtedly be amazed at the extent to which photographers have learned to make the medium speak and at the unique messages it conveys in today's society.

[1]Peter Henry Emerson, *Naturalistic Photography for Students of the Art* (1889; reprint, New York: Arno Press, 1973), p. 290.

[2]Wynn Bullock, *Photographing the Nude,* edited by Barbara Bullock-Wilson and Edna Bullock (Salt Lake City: Gibbs M. Smith, Inc., 1984), p. 80.

[3]Charles Baudelaire, "The Salon of 1859," *Art in Paris* 1845-1862, translated and edited by Jonathan Mayne (Oxford: Phaidon Press Ltd., 1981), p. 153.

[4] Brassaï, *Picasso and Company* (New York: Doubleday, 1966), pp. 46-47.

PHOTOGRAPHY SPEAKS

66 Photographers on Their Art

William Henry Fox Talbot
English, 1800 – 1877

Talbot's display, on January 25, 1839, of prints from the negative/positive process he formulated is generally regarded as the birth of conventional photography. Talbot patented his discovery in 1840 as the "calotype" process, and in 1844 he published *The Pencil of Nature,* the first book illustrated with actual photographic prints. His photographs were generally made in bright sunlight, which allowed exposure times of under one minute; despite this relatively fast exposure, most of Talbot's work consists of still lifes, architectural renderings and rural scenes. His reflection on how he came to invent this photographic process was originally published in *The Pencil of Nature.*

One of the first days of the month of October 1833, I was amusing myself on the lovely shores of the Lake of Como, in Italy, taking sketches with Wollaston's Camera Lucida, or rather I should say, attempting to take them: but with the smallest possible amount of success. For when the eye was removed from the prism — in which all looked beautiful — I found that the faithless pencil had only left traces on the paper melancholy to behold.

After various fruitless attempts, I laid aside the instrument and came to the conclusion, that its use required a previous knowledge of drawing, which unfortunately I did not possess.

I then thought of trying again a method which I had tried many years before. This method was, to take a Camera Obscura, and to throw the image of the objects on a piece of transparent tracing paper laid on a pane of glass in the focus of the instrument. On this paper the objects are distinctly seen, and can be traced on it with a pencil with some degree of accuracy, though not without much time and trouble. . . .

Such, then, was the method which I proposed to try again, and to endeavour, as before, to trace with my pencil the outlines of the scenery depicted on the paper. And this led me to reflect on the inimitable beauty of the pictures of nature's painting which the glass lens of the Camera throws upon the paper in its focus — fairy pictures, creations of a moment, and destined as rapidly to fade away.

It was during these thoughts that the idea occurred to me . . . how charming it would be if it were possible to cause these natural images to imprint themselves durably, and remain fixed upon the paper!

And why should it not be possible? I asked myself.

The picture, divested of the ideas which accompany it, and considered only in its ultimate nature, is but a succession or variety of stronger lights thrown upon one part of the paper, and of deeper shadows on another. Now Light, where it exists, can exert an action, and, in certain circumstances, does exert one sufficient to cause changes in material bodies. Suppose, then, such an action could be exerted on the paper; and suppose the paper could be visibly changed by it. In that case surely some effect must result having a general resemblance to the cause which produced it: so that the variegated scene of light and shade might leave its image or impression behind, stronger or weaker on different parts of the paper according to the strength or weakness of the light which had acted there.

Such was the idea that came into my mind. Whether it had ever occurred to me before amid floating philosophic visions, I know not, though I rather think it must have done so, because on this occasion it struck me so forcibly.

Building with Carriages, Paris, May 1843
Salt print, 6½″ x 6¾″

David Octavius Hill
Scottish, 1802 – 1870
Robert Adamson
Scottish, 1821 – 1848

Hill and Adamson are celebrated as the first successful painter/photographer collaborative team. Hill, a landscape painter and book illustrator, was commissioned to produce a massive group portrait (when finished in 1866, it measured eleven feet by five feet, and included 474 people), and he enlisted the photographic skills of Adamson to provide individual portraits from which he could paint. Hill posed and arranged the sitters, while Adamson handled the technicalities. The photographs remain excellent examples of the early use of William Henry Fox Talbot's calotype process; the close description of faces in bright sunlight demonstrates a prescient and clear understanding of the medium. In several of his letters, and in a prospectus for the photographs of Thomas Annan, Hill gave his thoughts and aspirations for the calotype.

It is worthy of notice, in passing, that the Portraits made chiefly for this Picture, in 1843 . . . by the then newly discovered Photographic Process of Mr Fox Talbot, called the Calotype or Talbotype, — Until then almost unknown or unapplied as a vehicle of artistic thought and expression, — were mainly the means of first raising the process to the rank of a Fine Art, or rather to that of one of its most magical and potent auxiliaries.

. . . The one selfish object I had in view in presenting them is gained, in their being in your library to demonstrate that we had at an early period of the art done it some service. I need not say I am otherwise more gratified in believing I have caused any gratification to the members of the Academy.

. . . The rough surface and unequal texture throughout of the paper is the main cause of the Calotype failing in details before the process of Daguerreotypes — and this is the very life of it. They look like the imperfect work of man — and not the much diminished perfect work of God.

. . . Our Academy have been making [illegible] important additions to their Library of late and I think this department will begin to receive more attention. They have received with [acceptance?] a project of mine to form a Calotype department of the Library of which I have formed the basis with 500 of my own. I think I have influence enough with not a few of the Calotypists to get copies of their best. These we propose to preserve in [beautiful?] volumes. Look one day to see this an important feature of our collection.

. . . I shall also see to your having a batch of calotypes — it may be some little time ere I can get them looked out — but it is a promise which shall gladly be redeemed. I am glad you have not tired of them. I had some hope the Chrystal Palace Fine Arts Jury would have awarded me a medal for my artistic application of this process — and I am still of the opinion they should have done so — it would have been some consolation for much time and money spent, I hope not foolishly, in making the art respectable.

Rev. Dr. William Maxwell Hetherington (1803-1865)
Professor of Apologetics and Systematic Theology at New College, Glasgow, ca. 1845
Salt print from calotype negative, 8″ x 5¾″

Anna Atkins
English, 1799 – 1871

Atkins is recognized as the first woman photographer. Before hearing of Fox Talbot's photographic reproduction process, Atkins made use of drawings, etchings and paintings to depict her interest in plant life. By using light-sensitized papers, however, Atkins was able to obtain precisely registered contact prints of botanical specimens, which she used to produce *Photographs of British Algae: Cyanotype Impressions* (1843) in a small edition — the first illustrative use of photographic images. Atkins, using handwritten text, explained her use of the new medium of photography:

The difficulty of making accurate drawings of objects so minute as many of the Algae and Confervae has induced me to avail myself of Sir John Herschel's beautiful process of Cyanotype, to obtain impressions of the plants themselves, which I have much pleasure in offering to my botanical friends.

I hope that <u>in general</u> the impressions will be found sharp and well defined, but in some instances/such as the Fuci/the thickness of the specimens renders it impossible to press the glass used in taking Photographs sufficiently close to them to insure a perfect representation of every part. Being however unwilling to omit any species to which I had access, I have preferred giving such impressions as I <u>could</u> obtain of these thick objects, to their entire omission. I take this opportunity of returning my thanks to the friends who have allowed me to use their collections of Algae on this occasion.

Aspidium Lobatum from *Cyanotypes of British and Foreign Flowering Plants and Ferns,* 1851-54
Cyanotype print, 13″ x 9¼″

Roger Fenton
English, 1819 – 1869

Woodcuts of Fenton's photographs of the Turkish/Russian conflict on the Crimean Peninsula (1854-1856), published in the *Illustrated London News,* provided the first extended documentation of war. Fenton attended school in France with the photographers Gustave LeGray, Charles Nègre and Henri LeSecq. In 1852 he was commissioned to photograph architecture and construction projects in Russia; the same year he assembled 800 pictures into the first exhibition of photographs in Great Britain. After the war he waged a successful campaign for the extension of copyright protection to photography. Fenton's sponsor to the Crimean conflict was the publisher of his photographs, William Agnew. Fenton's 1855 letters report:

Lord Raglan [Commander-in-the-Field of the British Army and Master-General of the Ordnance] was in town this morning with his staff. The soldiers have nothing but good words to say about him; one of them told me that when the weather was at the worst he was constantly sitting about amongst the men. . . .

I am now at Headquarters taking a few portraits I am yet in want of. Lord Raglan gave me a sitting this morning and I have obtained a very good likeness of him. General Pélissier, with whom I breakfasted this morning, is coming the day after tomorrow at five in the morning. It is impossible to work after nine or ten from the intense heat, which sends the stoppers flying out of my bottles, and spoils every picture. I am almost at the end of my materials, having only 1 oz. of nitrate of silver left. . . .

I have found a much better way of getting my van conveyed to the site I select than by applying to the authorities. As soon as a few of the prints had been seen, I was overwhelmed with applications to go here and there to take a portrait or a view of some tent or camp. If it is a place where I want to go, I go if they will drag the van up, and if it does not take me out of my way to Headquarters. For any very heavy pull the Artillery give me six horses for small distances; the men turn out in the hope of getting photographed in a group. This way I have travelled during the past week a great part of the way up, and had it not been pouring with rain I should have got there this evening. All the heavy part of my baggage not immediately needed I leave in my hut down here [Balaclava] where I print; the rest will be sent up by one of the railway wagons to the top of the hill and I shall have to cart it from there if I can borrow a cart, or carry it piecemeal on my horses by pack saddle.

Field Marshall Lord Raglan published by T. Agnew and Sons, November 1, 1855
Salt print, 7¾″ x 5⅞″

Maxime DuCamp
French, 1822 – 1894

DuCamp, a Parisian journalist and man-of-letters, made his only known photographs while traveling with the writer Gustave Flaubert through Greece, the Mid-East and Asia Minor between 1849 and 1851. Multiple sets of 125 albumen prints, made by the French photo-technician Louis-Dèsirè Blanquart-Evrard from DuCamp's negatives, were assembled into a travel album titled *Egypte, Nubie, Palestine et Syrie* (1852). This album, the first of its kind in France to use actual photographic prints in its presentation, brought DuCamp's straightforward impressions of exotic and fantastic regions home to the French public. While on his photographic expedition with Flaubert, DuCamp recorded his experiences in extensive notes.

Gustave gives a loud cry, and I am pale, my legs trembling. I cannot remember ever having been moved so deeply. . . . When we reached the Sphinx . . . Flaubert reined in his horse and cried, "I have seen the Sphinx fleeing toward Libya; it was galloping like a jackal." And he added: "That's from *Saint Anthony*. . . ."

Every time I visited a monument I had my photographic apparatus carried along and took with me one of my sailors, Hadji Ismael, an extremely handsome Nubian, whom I had climb up on to the ruins which I wanted to photograph. In this way I was always able to include a uniform scale of proportions. The great difficulty was to get Hadji Ismael to stand perfectly motionless while I performed my operations; and I finally succeeded by means of a trick whose success will convey the depth of naiveté of these poor Arabs. I told him that the brass tube of the lens jutting from the camera was a cannon, which would vomit a hail of shot if he had the misfortune to move — a story which immobilized him completely, as can be seen from my plates.

The day I was returning from Dendera I overheard the following conversation between him and Raïs Ibrahim — a curious account of a photographic expedition: "Well, Hadji Ismael, what news?" asked the *raïs* as we boarded the *cange*. "None," the sailor answered. "The Father of Thinness ('Abu Muknaf,' as I was called by my crew) ordered me to climb up on a column that bore the huge face of an idol; he wrapped his head in the black veil, he turned his yellow cannon towards me, then he cried: 'Do not move!' The cannon looked at me with its little shining eye, but I kept very still; and it did not kill me." "God is the greatest," said Raïs Ibrahim, sententiously. "And our Lord Mohammed is his prophet," replied Hadji.

Le Sphinx, 1849
Salt print, printed by Blanquart-Evard, 6⅛″ x 8⅛″

William Henry Jackson
American, 1843 – 1942

Jackson was one of the premier photographers of the western American frontier. Working with the cumbersome equipment necessary to make wet-plate negatives, Jackson documented the landscape charted by the United States Geological and Geographical Survey (1870-1878). His photographs from this period were instrumental in preserving the Yellowstone, Grand Teton and Mesa Verde areas as national parks. Jackson is also known for his portraits of American Indians and his commissioned images of railroad expansion in the West. These passages come from Jackson's autobiography, *Time Exposure,* published in 1940:

I wanted to have a large camera for certain pictures, and I picked a 20x24, that is, one taking a plate of 480 square inches — exactly twelve times the area of my 1874 negatives. No such camera was stocked in Washington; but I found one in New York, either at E. & H.T. Anthony's or the Scovill Manufacturing Co., as I remember. By late May of 1875 it was ready for me, and in the first week of June, I was on my way to Colorado with the largest camera I have ever handled outside of a studio. I can add that my 20x24 — although used only for exceptional shots — was worth all the extra labor it cost. . . .

[We] proceeded to Tower Creek. At the point where that stream drops into the gorge the view is magnificent — but recording it on a glass plate from the bed beneath turned out to be my biggest photographic problem of the year. Clambering down, and even up, the steep sides of the canyon was not an insuperable task. Neither was moving the camera over the same precipitous route. But getting the heavy dark box within working distance was a stickler. In fact, in the absence of mechanical aid, it couldn't be done.

Since the mountain could not be brought to Mohammed, another method had to be worked out, and finally I solved the situation. After setting up and focussing my camera at the bottom of the gorge, I would prepare a plate, back the holder with wet blotting paper, then slip and slide and tumble down to my camera and make the exposure. After taking my picture, I had to climb to the top carrying the exposed plate wrapped up in a moist towel. With Dixon to help, cleaning and washing the plates, I succeeded in repeating the procedure four or five times. The end of the day found us exhausted but very proud; and we had reason to be pleased with ourselves, for not a single one of our plates had dried out before being developed. . . .

Besides the riding horses I had six pack mules, four to carry grub, utensils, and tents, the remaining two to tote my cameras, chemicals, plates, and the same little orange-calico tent I had used in the Yellowstone. Everything was carried on aparejos, the stuffed-leather pack saddles commonly used in that country and farther south.

Hanging Rock, Clear Creek Canyon, Colorado, ca. 1875
Albumen print, 21¼″ x 17⅜″

Carleton E. Watkins
American, 1829 – 1916

Along with William Henry Jackson, Timothy O'Sullivan and other "frontier" photographers of the 1860s and 1870s, Watkins overcame the difficulties of cumbersome equipment and rough terrain to produce awe-inspiring views of the western American landscape. Accompanying various geological survey expeditions, Watkins photographed throughout California, Oregon and Nevada; in 1890 his images helped persuade Congress to set aside the Yosemite Valley as a national park. In letters to his wife, Frances, Watkins writes:

Anaconda, Saturday, July 5th, n.y.: Yesterday, "the glorious fourth," I started in to do some work and did do some altho the day was not satisfactory and today it is cloudy and raining, you can imagine in what humor I am in. Nearly a month gone and nothing done — the oldest inhabitant here never saw anything like it, but those that are not so old say the rainy season generally lasts until the 4th of July. This year is certainly no exception. If it was good weather I should have a tough job ahead of me and as it is it makes me pretty nearly sick and there is provocation enough without the weather.

Portland, Oregon, September 19, 1882: I never had the time seem so long to me on any trip that I ever made from home, and I am not half done my work, in fact barely commenced. It drags along awful slow, between the smoke and the rain and the wind, and as if the elements were not enough to worry me, a spark from an engine set fire to my [dark] tent last week and burned it half up, and it was the merest chance that it did not ruin the whole outfit. I was where I could not see it but some men working near called out to me and I got to it in time to prevent it doing any damage except to the tent. It took a couple of days to repair damages, and of course money. Talking about money. . . .

The North Dome, Yosemite, ca. 1866
Albumen print, 12¼″ x 8″

Eadweard Muybridge
American (b. England), 1830 – 1904

Primarily recognized for his studies of movement, Muybridge was also, during the 1860s, a widely traveled western landscape photographer; his work in Alaska and the western mountains demonstrates a dramatic and expressive style. But the bulk of his reputation lies in the thousands of sequential stop-motion images published in the eleven-volume *Animal Locomotion* (1887), photographs that convey information imperceptible to the unaided eye. An abridged version of that massive work was published in 1899 as *Animals in Motion*. In the preface of that book Muybridge wrote about his early experiments.

In the spring of the year 1872, while the author was directing the photographic surveys of the United States Government on the Pacific Coast, there was revived in the city of San Francisco a controversy in regard to animal locomotion, which we may infer, on the authority of Plato, was warmly argued by the ancient Egyptians, and which probably had its origin in the studio of the primitive artist when he submitted to a group of critical friends his first etching of a mammoth crushing through the forest, or of a reindeer grazing on the plains.

In this modern instance, the principal subject of dispute was the possibility of a horse, while trotting — even at the height of his speed — having all four of his feet, at any portion of his stride, simultaneously free from contact with the ground.

The attention of the author was directed to this controversy, and he immediately resolved to attempt its settlement.

The problem before him was, to obtain a sufficiently well-developed and contrasted image on a wet collodion plate, after an exposure of so brief a duration that a horse's foot, moving with a velocity of more than thirty yards in a second of time, should be photographed with its outlines practically sharp. . . .

Having constructed some special exposing apparatus, and bestowed more than usual care in the preparation of the materials he was accustomed to use for ordinarily quick work, the author commenced his investigation on the racetrack at Sacramento, California, in May, 1872, where he in a few days made several negatives of a celebrated horse named Occident, while trotting, laterally, in front of his camera, at rates of speed varying from two minutes and twenty-five seconds to two minutes and eighteen seconds per mile.

The photographs resulting from this experiment were sufficiently sharp to give a recognizable silhouette portrait of the driver, and some of them exhibited the horse with all four of his feet clearly lifted, at the same time, above the surface of the ground.

So far as the immediate point at issue was concerned, the object of the experiment was accomplished, and the question settled for once and for all time in favour of those who argued for a period of unsupported transit.

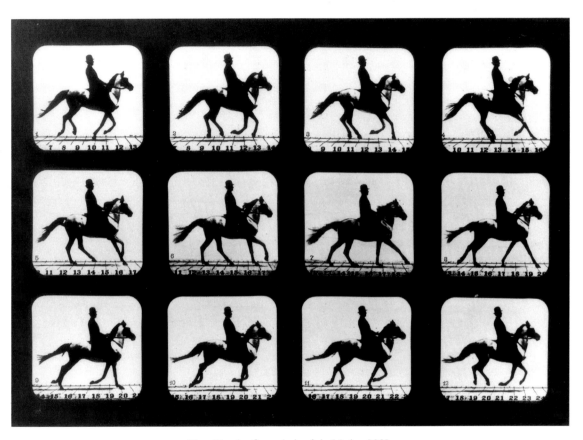

Horse Trotting from *Animals in Motion,* 1881
Albumen print, 5½″ x 9″

Lewis Carroll (Charles Lutwidge Dodgson)
English, 1832 – 1898

Although known primarily as the author of *Alice's Adventures in Wonderland* and *Through the Looking Glass,* Carroll is also regarded as one of the nineteenth century's greatest photographers of children. Like many of his contemporaries, Carroll found the new art of photography to be a stimulating avocation. In addition to his imaginative tableaux with children, Carroll proved himself as a highly capable photographic portraitist, depicting both adolescent and adult subjects. This satirical statement is excerpted from "A Photographer's Day Out," originally published in the *South Shields Amateur Magazine* in 1860.

They say that we Photographers are a blind race at best; that we learn to look at even the prettiest faces as so much light and shade; that we seldom admire, and never love. This is a delusion I long to break through — if I could only find a young lady to photograph, realizing my ideal of beauty — above all, if her name should be — (why is it, I wonder, that I dote on the name Amelia more than any other word in the English language?) — I feel sure that I could shake off this cold, philosophic lethargy.

The time has come at last. Only this evening I fell in with young Harry Glover in the Haymarket — "Tubbs!" he shouted, slapping me familiarly on the back, "my Uncle wants you down tomorrow at his Villa, camera and all!"

"But I don't know your Uncle," I replied, with my characteristic caution. (N.B. If I have a virtue, it is quiet, gentlemanly caution.)

"Never mind, old boy, he knows all about *you.* You be off by the early train, and take your whole kit of bottles, for you'll find lots of faces to uglify, and —"

"Ca'n't go," I said rather gruffly, for the extent of the job alarmed me, and I wished to cut him short, having a decided objection to talking slang in the public streets.

"Well, they'll be precious cut up about it, that's all," said Harry, with rather a blank face, "and my cousin Amelia —"

"Don't say another word!" I cried enthusiastically, "I'll go!"

Xie Kitchin, ca. 1870
Albumen print, 5½″ x 4″

Peter Henry Emerson
English (b. Cuba), 1856 – 1936

Emerson was an early and ardent champion of photographic purity; his 1889 book *Naturalistic Photography* argued for pictures that would replicate the in-person visual experience of a place. Emerson considered photography to be a blend of art and science, and his platinum prints and gravures of natural landscapes and rural genre scenes supported this theoretical stance. By 1899, however, he had tempered his views; a new edition of his book appeared with a final chapter entitled "Photography — Not Art," in which he recanted his previous stance and acquiesced to the popular preference for painterly manipulations. This statement appeared in the 1889 edition of *Naturalistic Photography*.

"A photograph," it has been said, "shows the art of nature rather than the art of the artist." This is mere nonsense, as the same remark might be applied equally well to all the fine arts. Nature does not jump into the camera, focus itself, expose itself, develop itself, and print itself. On the contrary, the artist, using photography as a medium, chooses his subject, selects his details, generalizes the whole in the way we have shown, and thus gives his view of nature. This is not copying or imitating nature, but interpreting her, and this is all any artist can do, and how perfectly he does it, depends on his technique, and his knowledge of this technique; and the resulting picture, by whatever method expressed, will be beautiful proportionately to the beauty of the original and the ability of the artist. These remarks apply equally to the critics who call pictures "bits of nature cut out." There is no need to slay the slain, and give any further answer to the objection that photography is a mechanical process, if there were, it would be enough to remind the objectors that if twenty photographers were sent to a district of limited area, and told to take a given composition, the result would be twenty different renderings. Photographs of any artistic quality have individuality as much as any other works of art. . . .

Photography has been called an "irresponsive medium." This is much the same as calling it a mechanical process, and, therefore, disposed of, we venture to think. A great paradox which has to be combatted, is the assumption that because photography is not "hand-work," as the public say, — though we find there is very much "hand-work *and* head-work" in it — therefore, it is not an Art language. This is a fallacy born of thoughtlessness. The painter learns his technique in order to speak, and as more than one painter has told us, "painting is a mental process," and as for the technique they could almost do that with their feet. So with photography, speaking artistically of it, it is a very severe mental process, and taxes all the artist's energies even after he has mastered his technique. The point is, *what you have to say,* and how to say it. It would be as reasonable to object to a poet printing his verse in type instead of writing it in old Gothic with a quill pen on asses' skin. Coupled with this accusation, goes that of want of originality. The originality of a work of art, it should be needless to say, refers to the originality of the thing expressed and the way it is expressed, whether it be in poetry, photography, or painting, and the original artist is surely he who seizes new and subtle impressions from nature, "tears them forth from nature," as Durer said, and lays them before the world by means of the technique at his command. That one technique is more difficult than another to learn, no one will deny, but the greatest thoughts have been expressed by means of the simplest technique — namely writing.

A Norfolk Boat-Yard from *Life and Landscape on the Norfolk Broads,* October 1886
Platinum print, 8¾″ x 11¼″

Eugène Atget
French, 1857 – 1927

Atget began to photograph at the age of forty, and became rapidly absorbed in a documentary project which, over the last thirty years of his life, resulted in more than ten thousand glass-plate negatives of turn-of-the-century Paris and its rural environs. His fame as a photographic artist has accrued entirely in retrospect; during his life he sold his photographs as reference works for artists in other media. Due to the efforts of Berenice Abbott and, more recently, the Museum of Modern Art, Atget's images are now considered early masterpieces of photographic realism. In 1920, concerned about the final disposition of his negatives, Atget wrote a letter to Monsieur Paul Léon, the Director of Fine Arts at Les Monuments Historiques, offering to sell his collection.

For more than twenty years, through my own labor and individual initiative, in all the venerable streets of Old Paris, I have been making photographic negatives measuring 18x24 cm, artistic documents of beautiful civil architecture from the 16th to the 19th century: the old mansions, houses historical or curious; beautiful facades, doorways, wainscots; door knockers, old fountains, period staircases (in wood and wrought iron); the interiors of all the churches of Paris (overall and artistic details: Notre-Dame, Saint-Gervais et Protais, Saint-Séverin, Saint-Julien-le-Pauvre, Saint-Etienne-du-Mont, Saint-Roch, Saint-Nicolas-du-Chardonnet, etc., etc.).

This enormous artistic and documentary collection is today complete. I can truthfully say that I possess all of Old Paris.

Now that I am approaching old age — that is to say, 70 years — and have neither heir nor successor, I am worried and tormented about the future of this beautiful collection of negatives, which could fall into hands unaware of its import and ultimately disappear, without benefitting anyone. I would be very happy Monsieur, if you could interest yourself in this collection. . . . I hold at your disposal, Monsieur, and with a simple word from you, my references on Old Paris and all the explanations you might wish to have from me.

Hotel de Parliamentarier, 3 Rue du Lions, ca. 1905
Albumen print, 8½″ x 7″

Frederick Evans
English, 1853 – 1943

Although Evans joined the Linked Ring Brotherhood in 1900, his work is more closely identified with photographic purism than with that group's pictorialist aesthetic. The Linked Ring was formed in London to promote photography as a fine art. They believed in making painterly photographs, which, because they looked like art, would be considered art. As a writer he campaigned for straight, unmanipulated prints and his luminous photographs of English and French architecture, influenced by Turner watercolors, have established Evans as perhaps the greatest architectural photographer. This statement is from a lecture given at the opening of Evans's exhibition at the Royal Photographic Society in London on April 25, 1900, as reprinted in *The Photographic Journal* of April 30, 1900.

My chief aim has always been to try for such effects of light and shade as will give the irresistible feeling that one *is* in an interior, and that it is full of light and space. Realism in the sense of true atmosphere, a feeling of space, truth of lighting, solidity and perfection of perspective (in the eye's habit of seeing it), has been my ambitious aim; and to say that I have not achieved it, but only hinted at it, would be praise enough, considering the really great difficulties in the way of a full achievement, and how few examples of such even the great "art world" can point to. . . .

I do not want to venture among those quicksands, the endless discussions as to whether photography can be considered in any degree art or fine art; but I would like just to hint that perhaps a more useful and a humbler way of looking at it would be as to why it should not be considered worthy a place among the crafts. A clever artistic photographer has a full claim I think to the cognomen craftsman. The great difficulty I have is in getting handworkers in any art to allow that I have any right to say or think that photography can be a means of expression. It is of course a very complete means of recording or copying, but of a personal art *expression* (which at times amounts to creative effort) they will hear nothing. They say that even though it may not always be done, yet it would be possible for six men to be sent to the same spot and to bring back the same camera record. This I deny. I contend there is as much individuality exercised in photographic as in any other work; those who oppose this could of course easily prove it for themselves by experimenting with a camera and half-a-dozen lenses, but this they will not do, and so the discussion gets limited to intelligent assertion on my part and ignorant assertion on theirs, and there is nothing so impossible or hopeless to combat as willful ignorance. I have often tried to repeat certain negatives, but have invariably failed, most so of course in out-of-door work: but even in interiors I think I might challenge any one to go to any of my subjects on these walls and bring away an exact replica, in print as well as negative of course: he may easily do better (or worse), but to repeat it with the so-called mechanical accuracy of the box with a glass in it is, I say, impossible, and if this does not mean individuality it means nothing, and individuality is the basis of all art. . . .

But now, to conclude this essay in the obvious, permit me to say, that even were I an artist in the accepted sense of the word, and making "art" my profession, I would rather be the producer of a good photograph than of a poor or indifferent painting or drawing; and I hope I shall never come to say, in parody of the proverb, "I cannot draw or paint, and to photograph I am ashamed."

Le Puy, Church of St. Michael D' Aiguilla, 1906-07
Platinum print, 9⅞" x 7¾"

Alfred Stieglitz
American, 1864 – 1946

Both as a photographer and an advocate, Stieglitz was one of the most important figures in twentieth century photography and art in general. In his own work, as in *Camera Work*, the influential magazine he founded and edited from 1902 until 1917, Stieglitz concentrated first on the emulation of painterly effects, then evolved into a clearer, less manipulative style in his portraits, urban studies, and landscapes. Considered "the father of modern photography," Stieglitz was instrumental in garnering acceptance for the medium. Stieglitz wrote the following statement for an exhibition of his photographs held at the Anderson Galleries, New York, in 1921:

My teachers have been life — work — continuous experiment. Incidentally a great deal of hard thinking. Any one can build on this experience with means available to all.

Many of my prints exist in one example only. Negatives of the early work have nearly all been lost or destroyed. There are but few of my early prints still in existence. Every print I make, even from one negative, is a new experience, a new problem. For, unless I am able to vary — add — I am not interested. There is no mechanicalization, but always photography.

My ideal is to achieve the ability to produce numberless prints from each negative, prints all significantly alive, yet indistinguishably alike, and to be able to circulate them at a price not higher than that of a popular magazine, or even a daily paper. To gain that ability there has been no choice but to follow the road I have chosen.

I was born in Hoboken. I am an American. Photography is my passion. The search for Truth is my obsession.

The Steerage, 1907
Photogravure, 12½″ x 10¼″

Alvin Langdon Coburn
English (b. America), 1882 – 1966

Mostly known for his mid-career Cubist-inspired "Vortographs" (regarded as the first purely abstract photographs), Coburn was also a prolific portraitist and urban landscape photographer. He produced more than 40,000 gravure prints for his books, which include *Men of Mark* (1913; British artists and literati), *New York* (1910), and *London* (1909). Coburn associated with both the English Pictorialist group, The Linked Ring, and Alfred Stieglitz's Photo Secession group in New York. Coburn was strongly affected by Whistler's paintings, Japanese rendering of tone and perspective and the urban imagery of Stieglitz. This statement is excerpted from "The Relation of Time to Art," originally published in *Camera Work* in 1908.

Photography is the most modern of the arts, its development and practical usefulness extends back only into the memory of living men; in fact, it is more suited to the art requirements of this age of scientific achievement than any other. It is, however, only by comparing it with the older art of painting that we will get the full value of our argument plainly before us; and in doing so we shall find that the essential difference is not so much a mechanical one of brushes and pigments as compared with a lens and dry plates, but rather a mental one of a slow, gradual, usual building up, as compared with an instantaneous, concentrated mental impulse, followed by a longer period of fruition. Photography born of this age of steel seems to have naturally adapted itself to the necessarily unusual requirements of an art that must live in skyscrapers, and it is because she has become so much at home in these gigantic structures that the Americans undoubtedly are the recognized leaders in the world movement of pictorial photography.

Just imagine anyone trying to paint at the corner of Thirty-fourth street, where Broadway and Sixth avenue cross! The camera has recorded an impression in the flashing fragment of a second. But what about the training, you will say, that has made this seizing of the momentary vision possible? It is, let me tell you, no easy thing to acquire, and necessitates years of practice and something of the instinctive quality that makes a good marksman. Just think of the combination of knowledge and sureness of vision that was required to make possible Stieglitz's "Winter on Fifth Avenue." If you call it a "glorified snapshot" you must remember that life has much of this same quality. We are comets across the sky of eternity.

The Two Trees, Rothenbergh, 1908
Photogravure, 14¾″ x 11″

Lewis Wickes Hine
American, 1874 – 1940

Educated as a sociologist, Hine employed photography for the cause of social reform. His most influential work was carried out in service of the National Child Labor Committee; his images of juveniles and children at work (1911-1916) were instrumental in changing labor regulations. In this work, and in photographs of Ellis Island immigrants, Red Cross efforts in Europe during World War I and the construction of the Empire State Building, Hine demonstrated respect and genuine personal concern for the conditions of his subjects; Hine's work stands as a model for social documentary photography. The following, entitled "Social Photography, How the Camera May Help in the Social Uplift," is excerpted from the *Proceedings of the National Conference of Corrections,* June 1909.

Whether it be a painting or a photograph, the picture is a symbol that brings one immediately into close touch with reality. It speaks a language learned early in the race and in the individual — witness the ancient picture writers and the child of today absorbed in his picture book. For us older children, the picture continues to tell a story packed into the most condensed and vital form. In fact, it is often more effective than the reality would have been, because, in the picture, the non-essential and conflicting interests have been eliminated. The picture is the language of all nationalities and all ages. The increase, during recent years, of illustrations in newspapers, books, exhibits and the like gives ample evidence of this.

The photograph has an added realism of its own; it has an inherent attraction not found in other forms of illustration. For this reason the average person believes implicitly that the photograph cannot falsify. Of course, you and I know that this unbounded faith in the integrity of the photograph is often rudely shaken, for, while photographs may not lie, liars may photograph. It becomes necessary, then, in our revelation of the truth, to see to it that the camera we depend upon contracts no bad habits.

Not long ago, a leader in social work, who had previously told me that photographs had been faked so much they were of no use to the work,

assured Editor Kellogg that the photographs of child labor in the Carolinas would stand as evidence in any court of law.

Moral: Despise not the camera, even though yellow-photography does exist.

With several hundred photos like those which I have shown, backed with records of observations, conversations, names and addresses, are we not better able to refute those who, either optimistically or hypocritically, spread the news that there is no child labor in New England?

Perhaps you are weary of child labor pictures. Well, so are the rest of us, but we propose to make you and the whole country so sick and tired of the whole business that when the time for action comes, child-labor pictures will be records of the past.

The artist, Burne-Jones, once said he should never be able to paint again if he saw much of those hopeless lives that have no remedy. What a selfish, cowardly attitude!

How different is the stand taken by Hugo, that the great social peril is darkness and ignorance, "What then," he says, "is required? Light! Light in floods!"

The dictum, then, of the social worker is "Let there be light;" and in this campaign for light we have for our advance agent the light writer — the photograph.

Picking Nut Meats, New York City, 1911
Gelatin-silver print, 10¼″ x 13¼″

Ansel Adams
American, 1902 – 1984

One of the world's most renowned photographers, and an empassioned spokesperson for both photography and nature preservation, Adams's early training as a musician voiced itself in the eloquent photographic orchestrations of landscape. His work in the early 1930s with the California-based Group f.64 helped develop and affirm photography as an autonomous medium. In his 1985 autobiography, Adams recalled the experience of producing his *Parmelian Prints* portfolio in the Spring of 1926:

. . . I was ushered into Albert's [Bender] office at 311 California Street. He was a partner in a leading insurance firm in the city, not large, but possessed of a remarkable clientele. His desk was a chaotic mass of letters, envelopes, postcards, books, and pamphlets: an ever-accumulating mound of memorabilia into which he could delve and immediately find whatever he sought. He greeted me warmly, talked a minute with his staff, made a phone call, then took me to a small table, pushed aside some books and periodicals, and said, "Let's look at them again." During his thorough inspection of my photographs he received at least two visitors and six phone calls, but nothing disturbed the intensity of his concentration on my work. After he finished, he looked me squarely in the eye and said, "We must do something with these photographs. How many of each can you print?"

I replied, "An unlimited number, unless I drop one of the glass plates."

He then said, "Let's do a portfolio." I remained outwardly calm, but was electrified by his decision.

We quickly established the probable costs and the time required to do the job. He called Jean Chambers Moore, a respected publisher and dealer in fine books, and arranged for her to publish the portfolio and the Grabhorn Press to do the typography as well as the announcement. Edwin and Robert Grabhorn had developed a worldwide reputation for their incredibly beautiful typographic design and printing. Having decided upon an edition of one hundred portfolios (and ten artist's copies) of eighteen prints each, Albert suggested a retail price of fifty dollars for each portfolio. It was a whirlwind morning. This was my first experience with such decisive organization; red tape was not a part of Albert's world. . . .

Jean Chambers Moore decided she dare not publish the portfolio if it had the term *photographs* in the title. She was adamant against my objections; she was the experienced publisher, not I. We needed to sell the remaining half of the portfolios, and at that time creative photography was not considered commercially viable, as hardly anyone considered it to be a fine art. Hence, we coined a bastard word to take the place of photograph — *Parmelian Prints.* I am not proud at allowing this breach of faith in my medium. And then, to add to my chagrin, when I saw the finished title page I found an error, *Parmelian Prints of the High Sierras.* The name *Sierra* is already a plural. To add an *s* is a linguistic, Californian, and mountaineering sin.

Mount Brewer and Bullfrog Lake, Kings Canyon National Park from *Parmelian Prints of the High Sierras,* ca. 1925
Gelatin-silver print, 5¾″ x 7¾″

Imogen Cunningham
American, 1883 – 1976

Through an active career spanning 65 years, Cunningham emerged from an early painterly attitude instilled by Pictorialist Gertrude Käsebier to become one of the pioneers of West Coast modernism. Her best known work, voluptuously detailed close-up renditions of plants and flowers, linked her with the purist Group f.64 in the 1930s. At the time of her death she was involved in a portraiture project on elderly people, published as *After Ninety* (1977). In a 1961 interview conducted by Edna Tartaul Daniel for the Regional Cultural History Project at the University of California, Berkeley, Cunningham said:

Of course I think a good many people go into photography because they think it's easy. The ones who succeed don't think that, but people go into it thinking like the old slogan that Eastman Company put out, "You press the button and we do the rest."

For one thing, I think that people like the freedom of photography whether they are women or men. You can be your own boss. . . .

I wasn't very ambitious. I think that's the solution. I just took things as they came. I wouldn't say I didn't have any problem, but I didn't care. I didn't think I was going to save the world by doing photography as some of these people do. I just was having a good time doing it, and so I still had a good time no matter what I had to photograph, so I photographed the plants in my garden and steered my children around at the same time.

But I can think of the times we went into the mountains and into the Southwest when, if I had had a little camera, I would have done a lot more work than I did. I didn't have anything but a big camera, and the big camera and the children were just too much for me. . . .

I have no ambition, never did have any ambition to be a reporter. That is something different. I still feel that my interest in photography has something to do with the [a]esthetic, and that there should be a little beauty in everything.

Triangles, 1928
Gelatin-silver print, 3¾″ x 2¾″

Paul Strand
American, 1890 – 1976

One of the principal exponents of photographic modernism, Strand was closely associated with Stieglitz in the 1910s and 1920s; Stieglitz devoted the last two issues of *Camera Work* to Strand's undiluted images of architecture, still lifes and candid street portraiture. During the 1930s Strand was active as a filmmaker, but returned full-time to photography in the 1940s, extending his reputation as a master photographer and impeccable printer. Strand's *Time in New England* (1950) is considered one of the great books of American photography. Strand's statement was originally published in *Seven Arts,* 1917.

Photography, which is the first and only important contribution thus far, of science to the arts, finds its *raison d'être,* like all media, in a complete uniqueness of means. This is an absolute unqualified objectivity. Unlike the other arts which are really anti-photographic, this objectivity is of the very essence of photography, its contribution and at the same time its limitation. And just as the majority of workers in other media have completely misunderstood the inherent qualities of their respective means, so photographers, with the possible exception of two or three, have had no conception of the photographic means. The full potential power of every medium is dependent upon the purity of its use, and all attempts at mixture end in such dead things as the color-etching, the photographic painting and in photography, the gum-print, oil-print, etc., in which the introduction of hand work and manipulation is merely the expression of an impotent desire to paint. It is this very lack of understanding and respect for their material, on the part of photographers themselves which directly accounts for the consequent lack of respect on the part of the intelligent public and the notion that photography is but a poor excuse for an inability to do anything else.

The photographer's problem therefore, is to see clearly the limitations and at the same time the potential qualities of his medium, for it is precisely here that honesty, no less than intensity of vision, is the prerequisite of a living expression. This means a real respect for the thing in front of him, expressed in terms of chiaroscuro (color and photography having nothing in common) through a range of almost infinite tonal values which lie beyond the skill of human hand. The fullest realization of this is accomplished without tricks of process or manipulation, through the use of straight photographic methods. It is in the organization of this objectivity that the photographer's point of view toward Life enters in, and where a formal conception born of the emotions, the intellect, or of both, is as inevitably necessary for him, before an exposure is made, as for the painter, before he puts brush to canvas. The objects may be organized to express the causes of which they are the effects, or they may be used as abstract forms, to create an emotion unrelated to the objectivity as such. This organization is evolved either by movement of the camera in relation to the objects themselves or through their actual arrangement, but here, as in everything, the expression is simply the measure of a vision, shallow or profound as the case may be. Photography is only a new road from a different direction but moving toward the common goal, which is Life.

Iris, Georgetown, Maine, 1928
Gelatin-silver print 9½″ x 7½″

André Kertész
American (b. Hungary), 1894 – 1985

Kertész was one of the first photographic artists to fully avail himself of the small format camera. His work, including portraits, still lifes, reportage and experimental abstractions, reflects a curiosity in and a passion for serendipitous moments in life. Although he was widely respected as an influence and a mentor in France, where he lived from 1925 to 1936, recognition in the United States was long delayed; publishers during the 1940s and 1950s considered his images too subtle and eloquent. While living in Paris, his work was closely linked with the development of surrealism. This statement is taken from a May 1982 unpublished interview.

I am not surrealist. I am only realist. All this group — surrealists — use my name. No, no, I am realist. Not surrealist. You can give any explanation [that] you want, this is a normal realist thing that I do. . . . I did the same in Budapest before the surrealist. . . . All the so-called element [that] you find later, the so-called modern business. . . . I did before, without knowing surrealism . . . [there] was no surrealism in this time. I lived in Paris in this day, but I had material before. People give [it] a new name, that's all. . . .

And come a crazy photographer . . . you know, in the infantry you have everything in your rucksack. Very heavy. Lose my glass plate, lose my metal holder, you can imagine. The idea was if I stay alive. . . . Fine with me and that's that. Now in the end I stay alive. . . . And in Esztergom made my first distortion, underwater . . . we [were] sitting around in the pool, talking before lunch . . . everybody was wounded . . . we [were] the wounded men. And we [were] sitting around talking and in the water [was] the leg. The hand. And I began shooting this. "You are crazy; what you are doing?" [they asked me.] I made I don't know how many [photographs] for the girlfriends; for your girlfriend the face is interesting. . . . We make the joke [that] I am crazy. And this was effectively the beginning of distortion photography. . . .

And the *Pipe and Glasses*. It was between talk. Between talk over these things I make the photo, that's all. Something like that. Look I don't make again very little. Except one photo or two. No really, this is what is going around now, shooting a thousand for one, but I didn't make [*Pipe and Glasses*] that way. If you know what you want to do, you don't make thousand. Or a hundred. . . . If you feel exactly what you want and you have your technique, [and you are] not playing around, [it] is unnecessary. Pipe was one shot. We worked in glass plate, you don't go around with [a] hundred.

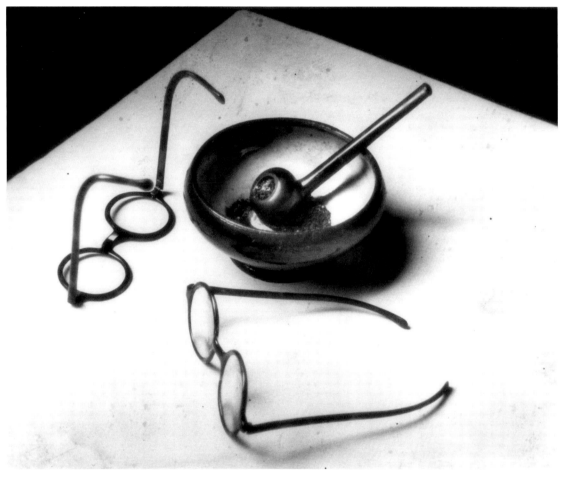

Pipe and Glasses, Paris, 1926
Gelatin-silver print, 7¾″ x 9¾″

László Moholy-Nagy
American (b. Austria-Hungary), 1895 – 1946

Although he didn't commonly refer to himself as a photographer (he was also involved in painting, sculpture and stage design), Moholy-Nagy influenced both the practice and the conception of the medium. His photography explored new perspectives through the use of both high and low viewpoints and experimental methods of collage and montage. He was also active as a theoretician, serving on the faculty of the German Bauhaus and its post-1937 incarnation as the Chicago Institute of Design, where he set a precedent for graduate-level photography teaching. This statement is from a much longer text entitled "From Pigment to Light" originally published in *Telehor* in 1936.

The New Vision

All interpretations of photography have hitherto been influenced by the aesthetic-philosophic concepts that circumscribed painting. These were for long held to be equally applicable to photographic practice. Up to now, photography has remained in rather rigid dependence on the traditional forms of painting; and like painting it has passed through the successive stages of all the various art "isms"; though in no sense to its advantage. Fundamentally new discoveries cannot for long be confined to the mentality and practice of bygone periods with impunity. When that happens all productive activity is arrested. This was plainly evinced in photography, which has yielded no results of any value except in those fields where, as in scientific work, it has been employed without artistic ambitions. Here alone did it prove the pioneer of an original development, or of one peculiar to itself.

In this connection it cannot be too plainly stated that it is quite unimportant whether photography produces "art" or not. Its own basic laws, not the opinions of art critics, will provide the only valid measure of its future worth. It is sufficiently unprecedented that such a "mechanical" thing as photography, and one regarded so contemptuously in an artistic and creative sense, should have acquired the power it has, and become one of the primary objective visual forms, in barely a century of evolution. Formerly the painter impressed his own perspective outlook on his age. We have only to recall the manner in which we used to look at landscapes, and compare it with the way we perceive them now! Think, too, of the incisive sharpness of those camera portraits of our contemporaries, pitted with pores and furrowed by lines. Or an air-view of a ship at sea moving through waves that seem frozen in light. Or the enlargement of a woven tissue, or the chiselled delicacy of an ordinary sawn block of wood. Or, in fact, any of the whole gamut of splendid details of structure, texture, and "factor" of whatever objects we care to choose.

Waterfront, Turku, Finland, early 1930s
Gelatin-silver print, 9¼" x 7"

Laura Gilpin
American, 1891–1979

In her book *The Enduring Navaho* (1968), Gilpin's lifelong project involving places and indigenous people of the American Southwest came to fruition. Having attended the Clarence White School in New York from 1916 to 1918, she relocated to Santa Fe, New Mexico in 1946 and began to focus on the Navaho Indians and the Canyon de Chelly region, supporting her project with portrait commissions and commercial assignments. This statement was originally published in the journal *Ninety-Eight-Six,* May 1928.

Since the invention of the [K]odak, photography has become immensely popular. And here lies one grave danger. Everybody thinks it is easy! Two well known advertisements have not in the least helped matters. "It's all in the lens" and "You push the button we do the rest" sound marvelous. But — is it all in the lens? The quickest answer to this would be to show you some wonderful examples of pin hole photography when the negatives were made without any lens at all, just a fine needle hole in a piece of black paper. After all is said and done it isn't what kind of a lens or camera you have, it is what kind of a picture you make with that lens and camera. This requires much thought, much study, much knowledge. It has often been said that the camera is a machine therefore its results must be mechanical. This is far indeed from the truth. The photographer makes his negative not with his hand but with his brain. As a matter of fact there is nothing so extremely sensitive as the camera. It can record the greatest delicacies of line and tone, and in portraiture the most subtle expressions. When photography gains artists who are equally sensitive, are skilled in their technique, and big in their perceptions, then we will have monumental works of art.

Every great work of art is fundamentally a fine design in its arrangement of light and dark, of line and form. All of us are sensitive to this, some of [us] consciously, some unconsciously. The photographer can arrange his picture just as the painter does, only sometimes he must go about it in a different way. The greatest tool at our command is the very thing that IS photography. LIGHT. Light is our paint brush and it is a most willing tool in the hands of the one who studies it with sufficient care. It seems to me that too often this all important factor of our work is overlooked. Choosing the right light for a given subject is vital to the success of your picture. Failing to do this, you simply have a record of facts. These are the elements of your photograph and on them rests your success, the lighting you choose, and the way you arrange your masses of dark and light tones on the plate.

Then we come to the making of the print, skipping momentarily the intermediate technical step of developing the negative. The highest ideals of a print are one of quality. Quality of tone, of texture. . . . One of the great allurements of photography is the many different kinds of printing processes from which we may choose. You can take the same negative and secure a half a dozen different effects by the use of a different process. . . . In fact one of the greatest problems is finding time to do all the many interesting things there are to do in this work.

Bryce Canyon #2, 1930
Platinum print, 9½″ x 7½″

Walker Evans
American, 1903 – 1975

Evans was responsible for the emergence in 1930s American photography of a new, more literary, less dramatic conception of documentary description. Drawing upon the work of Atget, Evans made head-on, highly detailed images of Americans and the material manifestations of their indigenous cultures. He was employed by the Farm Security Administration project from 1935 to 1938; his work has appeared in several important books, including *American Photographs* (1938) and *Let Us Now Praise Famous Men* (1941) on which he collaborated with the writer James Agee. This statement is from an interview by Leslie Katz, published in the March-April 1971 *Art in America*.

It's logical to say that what I do is an act of faith. Other people might call it conceit, but I have faith and conviction. It came to me. And I worked it out. I used to suffer from a lack of it, and now that I've got it I suppose it seems self-centered. I have to have faith or I can't act. I think what I am doing is valid and worth doing, and I use the word *transcendent*. That's very pretentious, but if I'm satisfied that something transcendent shows in a photograph I've done, that's it. It's there, I've done it. Without being able to explain, I know it absolutely, that it happens sometimes, and I know by the way I feel in the action that it goes like magic — this is it. It's as though there's a wonderful secret in a certain place and I can capture it. Only I can do it at this moment, only this moment and only me. That's a hell of a thing to believe, but I believe it or I couldn't act. It's a very exciting, heady thing. It happens more when you're younger, but it still happens, or I wouldn't continue. I think there is a period of esthetic discovery that happens to a man and he can do all sorts of things at white heat. Yeats went through three periods. T.S. Eliot was strongest in his early period, I think. E.E. Cummings seemed to go on without losing much. After all, poetry is art and these fields are related. It's there and it's a mystery and it's even partly mystical and that's why it's hard to talk about in a rational, pragmatic society. But art goes on. . . . The unappreciated artist is at once very humble and very arrogant too. He collects and edits the world about him. This is especially important in the psychology of camera work. This is why a man who has faith, intelligence and cultivation will show it in his work. Fine photography is literate, and it should be. It does reflect cultivation if there *is* cultivation. This is also why, until recently, photography has had no status, as it's usually practiced by uncultivated people. I always remember telling my classes that the students should seek to have a cultivated life and an education: they'd make better photographs. On the other hand, Eugène Atget was an uneducated man, I think, who was a kind of medium, really. He was like Blake. His work sang like lightning through him. He could infuse the street with his own poetry, and I don't think he even was aware of it or could articulate it. What I've just been saying is not entirely true. Since I'm a half-educated and self-educated man, I believe in education. I do note that photography, a despised medium to work in, is full of empty phonies and worthless commercial people. That presents quite a challenge to the man who can take delight in being in a very difficult, disdained medium.

Untitled, ca. 1930
Gelatin-silver print, 4⅝″ x 3″

Man Ray (Emmanuel Radnitsky)
American, 1890 – 1976

Just as Man Ray was influenced by his associations with DuChamp, Dadaism, Cubism and Surrealism, so were his own artworks difficult to categorize. He made photographs, films, paintings and found-object sculptures with interchangeable fluency and innovative skill. Within photography, his series of Rayograms — objects placed on photographic paper and exposed to light — and solarized portraits distinguished him as one of the medium's unique, iconoclastic talents. This excerpt is from "Photography is Not Art," published in the book *Man Ray Photographs*.

. . . I ask you, how can we ever get together on the question of beauty? This dilemma fortunately no longer troubles a self-respecting Artist. In fact, to him the word beauty has become a red rag, and with reason. I am not being sarcastic, but mean it in all sincerity, when I say that the Artist even when copying another, works under the illusion that he is covering ground which he imagines no one has covered before him. He is then necessarily discovering a new beauty which only he can appreciate, to begin with. (In this respect he really returns to nature, because he employs her time-honored mode of repetition, unconsciously. Only the desire to make a permanent work is conscious.) Aside from this, *the success with which the Artist is able to conceal the source of his inspiration, is the measure of his originality*. The final defense is, of course, "I paint what I like," meaning he paints what he likes most, or he paints that which he fears, or which is beyond his attainments, in the hope of mastering it. . . .

It was a mere hazard that photography began with the black and white image, perhaps it was even fortunate for the possibilities of a new art, or that a new art might become possible. The violent attacks by painters on photography were mitigated by its lack of color of which they still had the monopoly, and they could afford a certain indul-

gence. Just as in writing, "l'humeur noir" had been considered the bastard child, a new black and white graphic medium could never be feared as a serious competitor. But, if this humor should assume all the colored facets of a serious form, like the present discourse, or if a photograph should break out into all the colored growths accessible to the painter, then the situation would indeed become serious for the exclusive painter. Then the danger of photography becoming a succeeding art, instead of simply another art, would be imminent. Or rather, the danger of photography becoming simply Art instead of remaining AN art. To complete this result, a little research and some determination could prove that whatever was possible in the plastic domain, was equally feasible in the optical domain. The trained human eye, guiding one of glass, could capture as wide a field as had been controlled by a more or less trained hand guided by a half-closed eye.

To conclude, nothing is sadder than an old photograph, nothing so full of that nostalgia so prized by many of our best painters, and nothing so capable of inspiring us with that desire for a true Art, as we understand it in painting. When photography will have lost that sourness, and when it will age like Art or alcohol, only then will it become Art and not remain simply AN art as it is today.

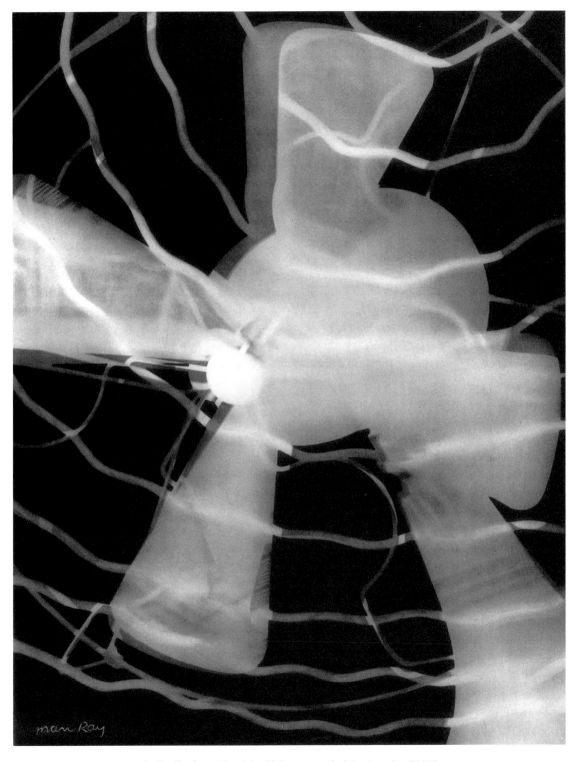

Le Souffle, from *Electricite, 10 Rayograms by Man Ray,* April 1931
Photogravure, 10¼" x 8"

Henri Cartier-Bresson
French, 1908 –

Cartier-Bresson's spontaneous photographs, cross-sections of life framed with a hand-held camera, embody the concept of "the decisive moment" (the title of his 1952 book). Although he was involved in the forming of the important photojournalistic agency Magnum (1947), his work in China, India, France, the United States and elsewhere is concerned more with a singular photographic beauty than with specific reportage. Cartier-Bresson has also been deeply interested in painting and film and has pursued these media along with his influential photography. This statement is from the introduction to Cartier-Bresson's 1952 book *The Decisive Moment*.

The photographer's eye is perpetually evaluating. A photographer can bring coincidence of line simply by moving his head a fraction of a millimeter. He can modify perspectives by a slight bending of the knees. By placing the camera closer to or farther from the subject, he draws a detail — and it can be subordinated, or he can be tyrannized by it. But he composes a picture in very nearly the same amount of time it takes to click the shutter, at the speed of a reflex action.

Sometimes it happens that you stall, delay, wait for something to happen. Sometimes you have the feeling that here are all the makings of a picture — except for just one thing that seems to be missing. But what one thing? Perhaps someone suddenly walks into your range of view. You follow his progress through the view-finder. You wait and wait, and then finally you press the button — and you depart with the feeling (though you don't know why) that you've really got something. Later, to substantiate this, you can take a print of this picture, trace on it the geometric figures which come up under analysis, and you'll observe that, if the shutter was released at the decisive moment, you have instinctively fixed a geometric pattern without which the photograph would have been both formless and lifeless.

Composition must be one of our constant preoccupations, but at the moment of shooting it can stem only from our intuition, for we are out to capture the fugitive moment, and all the interrelationships involved are on the move. In applying the Golden Rule, the only pair of compasses at the photographer's disposal is his own pair of eyes. Any geometrical analysis, any reducing of the picture to a schema, can be done only (because of its very nature) after the photograph has been taken, developed, and printed — and then it can be used only for a post-mortem examination of the picture. I hope we will never see the day when photoshops sell little schema grills to clamp onto our viewfinders; and the Golden Rule will never be found etched on our ground glass.

If you start cutting or cropping a good photograph, it means death to the geometrically correct interplay of proportions. Besides, it very rarely happens that a photograph which was feebly composed can be saved by reconstruction of its composition under the darkroom's enlarger; the integrity of vision is no longer there. There is a lot of talk about camera angles; but the only valid angles in existence are the angles of the geometry of composition and not the ones fabricated by the photographer who falls flat on his stomach or performs other antics to procure his effects.

Rue Mouffetard, Paris, 1954
Gelatin-silver print, 14″ x 9½″

Hans Bellmer
German, 1902 – 1975

Trained as a technical artist and graphic designer, Bellmer merged the detail-orientation of these disciplines with a fantasy realm derived from childhood escapism and the darkly expressionist art and theater of early 1930s Europe. In 1933 he began to create and photograph a bizarre series of dolls, entitled "poupée," which eventually formed the core of his work. Upon settling in Paris in 1938, Bellmer was affiliated with the Surrealist movement, and his images were often used as illustrations in surrealist publications. In his 1962 book *Die Puppe,* Bellmer outlined his theories for this style of working.

Like everyone, I was born with a very pronounced need for "comfort," for a paradisiacal and limitless indolence. But limits were very quickly laid down for me, in the form of "father" and a little later in the form of "policeman." Beyond the warm and delicate presence of my mother, there was the hostile masculine authority: the enemy, the frustrator (detainer) of power. . . .

The body is like a phrase that invites us to disjoint it (to pull it apart), so that it can be recomposed through an infinite series of anagrams [which is] its true content. . . . an artificial woman of anatomical possibilities [which are] capable of reshaping the giddiness of passion into the invention of desire. . . .

Like the gardener who compels the boxwood to take the shape of a ball, cone, cube, so man imposes on the image of woman his elementary certainties, the geometric and algebraic habits of his thought.

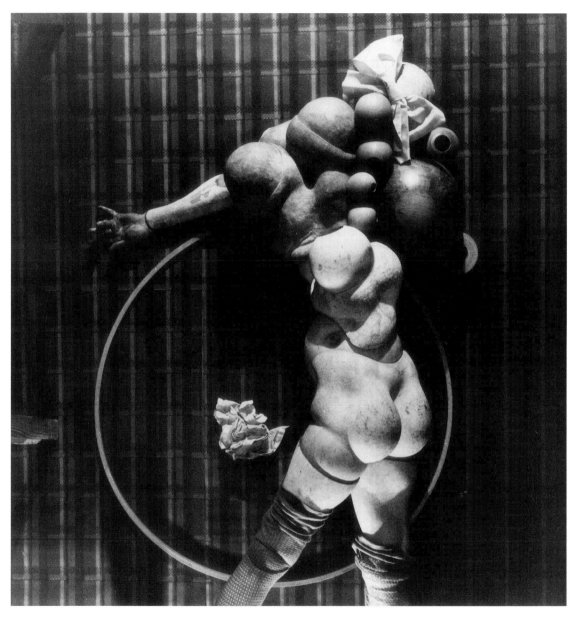

La Poupée, 1935
Gelatin-silver print, 9¾″ x 9⅜″

August Sander
German, 1876 – 1964

Sander's portraits were intended to provide a cross-section of the German "Volk" during the 1920s. His book *Antlitz der Zeit* (Face of the Time, 1929) was the first volume of an extended series which, Sander hoped, would have provided an exhaustive catalog of all classes and types in Germany; however, his factual documentation contradicted the Aryan ideals of the rising Nazi Party, and his work was banned in the early 1930s. At that point, he turned his camera to landscapes. This statement comes from an essay written in 1927 to formally announce Sander's project, "Man of the Twentieth Century." The occasion was an exhibition of modern painting, sculpture and photography sponsored by the Cologne Art Association.

People often ask me how I came upon the idea of creating this work: seeing, observing, and thinking — and the question is answered. Nothing seemed to me more appropriate than to project an image of our time with absolute fidelity to nature by means of photography. We find writings and books with illustrations from all ages, but photography has provided us with new possibilities and tasks, different from those of painting. It can reproduce things with grandiose beauty, but also with cruel truthfulness; and it can also deceive incredibly. We must be able to endure seeing the truth, but above all we should pass it on to our fellow men and to posterity, whether it be favorable or unfavorable for us. Now if I, as a healthy human being, am so immodest as to see things as they are and not as they are supposed to be or can be, then I beg your pardon, but I can't act differently. I have been a photographer for thirty years and have engaged in photography with the utmost seriousness; I have taken good paths and bad paths, and recognized my errors. The exhibit at the Cologne Art Association is the result of my search, and I hope that I am now on the right path. Nothing is more hateful to me than photography sugar-coated with gimmicks, poses, and false effects. Therefore, let me speak the truth in all honesty about our age and the people of our age.

Businessman, Linz, Rhine, 1930
Gelatin-silver print, 9⅛″ x 6¾″

Brassaï (Gyula Halász)
French (b. Transylvania), 1899 –1984

Brassaï's images of Parisian street and night life, populated with underworld and underground characters, have come to epitomize the darkly romantic Paris of the 1930s. He was encouraged by his friend André Kertész to take up photography after finding painting lacking in immediacy. Brassaï associated with the Surrealists, and his book *Paris de Nuit* (1933) has become a classic example of personal, interpretive documentation. Brassaï wrote of his experiences photographing for that book.

During my first years in Paris, beginning in 1924, I lived at night, going to bed at sunrise, getting up at sunset, wandering about the city from Montparnasse to Montmartre. And even though I had always ignored and even disliked photography before, I was inspired to become a photographer by my desire to translate all the things that enchanted me in the nocturnal Paris I was experiencing. So *Paris de Nuit,* published in 1933, was born. . . .

The real night people, however, live at night not out of necessity, but because they want to. They belong to the world of pleasure, of love, vice, crime, drugs. A secret, suspicious world, closed to the uninitiated. Go at random into one of those seemingly ordinary bars in Montmartre, or into a dive in the Goutte-d'Or neighborhood. Nothing to show they are owned by clans of pimps, that they are often the scenes of bloody reckonings. Conversation ceases. The owner looks you over with an unfriendly glance. The clientele sizes you up: this intruder, this newcomer — is he an informer, a stool pigeon? Has he come in to blow the gig, to squeal? You may not be served, you may even be asked to leave, especially if you try to take pictures. . . . And yet, drawn by the beauty of evil, the magic of the lower depths, having taken pictures for my "voyage to the end of night" from the outside, I wanted to know what went on inside, behind the walls, behind the façades, in the wings: bars, dives, night clubs, one-night hotels, bordellos, opium dens. I was eager to penetrate this other world, this fringe world, the secret, sinister world of mobsters, outcasts, toughs, pimps, whores, addicts, inverts. Rightly or wrongly, I felt at the time that this underground world represented Paris at its least cosmopolitan, at its most alive, its most authentic, that in these colorful faces of its underworld there had been preserved, from age to age, almost without alteration, the folklore of its most remote past.

Une Fille de Joie, Boulevard Rochechouart, Montmartre, 1932
Gelatin-silver print, 8⅞″ x 6⅞″

Bill Brandt
English, 1904 – 1983

After studying with Man Ray in Paris in the early 1930s, Brandt returned to England and, over the next forty years, created a singular body of work that has identified him as Britain's most important photographer of this century. Although exposed to Surrealism, Brandt's moody, evocative landscapes, portraits, nude studies and domestic tableaux reveal a unique sensibility imbued with inventive and iconoclastic romanticism. In his 1948 book, *Camera in London,* Brandt delivered his Photographer's Credo:

. . . I did not always know just what it was I wanted to photograph. I believe it is important for a photographer to discover this, for unless he finds what it is that excites him, what it is that calls forth at once an emotional response, he is unlikely to achieve his best work. For me it was not easy. Simply because my response was so much a matter of instinct that consciously I could not formulate it. In fact I did not try to do so. I now have through experience a more conscious knowledge of what it is that excites me — or would it be more exact to say of what does not excite me? Yet instinct itself should be a strong enough force to carve its own channel. Too much self-examination or self-consciousness about it or about one's aims and purposes may in the early stages be a hindrance rather than a help.

If his instinct did not guide him, either consciously or subconsciously, a photographer might work for years without experiencing the excitement of creative work with his camera. To discover what it is that quickens his interest and emotional response is particularly difficult for the photographer to-day because advances in technical equipment have made it possible to take such a wide variety of subjects under such varying conditions that the choice before him has become immense in its scope. The good photographer will produce a competent picture every time whatever his subject. But only when his subject makes an immediate and direct appeal to his own interests will he produce work of distinction. . . .

It is part of the photographer's job to *see* more intensely than most people do. He must have and keep in him something of the receptiveness of the child who looks at the world for the first time or of the traveller who enters a strange country. Most photographers would feel a certain embarrassment in admitting publicly that they carried within them a sense of wonder, yet without it they would not produce the work they do, whatever their particular field. It is the gift of seeing the life around them clearly and vividly, as something that is exciting in its own right. It is an innate gift, varying in intensity with the individual's temperament and environment. . . .

By temperament I am not unduly excitable and certainly not *trigger-happy.* I think twice before I shoot and very often do not shoot at all. By professional standards I do not waste a lot of film; but by the standards of many of my colleagues I probably miss quite a few of my opportunities. Still, the things I am after are not in a hurry as a rule. I am a photographer of London.

Parlormaid and Under-Parlormaid Ready to Serve Dinner, ca. 1933
Gelatin-silver print, 9″ x 7¾″

Weegee (Arthur H. Fellig)
American (b. Austria-Hungary), 1899 – 1968

Arthur H. Fellig derived his "nom de foto" from his uncanny Ouija board-like ability (later abetted by a police radio) to sense and be present at scenes of urban calamities almost as they happened. "Weegee the Famous," as his credit line read, became known in the 1930s and 1940s for his raw, spontaneous photographs of victims, survivors and onlookers at crime scenes and fires in New York City. Weegee was also concerned with documenting more humane, humorous urban situations; after the publication of his New York work in *Naked City* (1945) he turned to photographs of Hollywood culture and experiments with distorting lenses. His egocentric personality is revealed in this statement from *Weegee by Weegee: An Autobiography*, 1961.

On my safaris and lecture tours all over the world, people were always asking for the secret of my success. (Thanks for the compliment.) It's very simple. I've just been myself. Besides, I was born with a great inferiority complex and just had to make good, giving all my life and energy to my work. I'm no part-time dilettante photographer, unlike the bartenders, shoe salesmen, floorwalkers, plumbers, barbers, grocery clerks and chiropractors whose great hobby is their camera. All their friends rave about what wonderful pictures they take. If they're so good, why don't they take pictures full-time, for a living, and make floorwalking, chiropractics, etc., their hobby? But everyone wants to play it safe. They're afraid to give up their pay checks and their security . . . they might miss a meal. . . .

The camera is the modern Aladdin's lamp. It has given me all the things I've wanted . . . fame, fortune and friends. It is the easiest profession to get into because editors are always looking for something human, something different. The doors are always open to beginners and unknowns. Other photographers think the magic name of Weegee hypnotized the editors into buying my pictures. That's not so. To prove it, I tried a little experiment in London. Unannounced, and without an appointment, I went to *The Times*. They had never heard of me, much to my amazement (I amaze

easily). I showed them some of my kaleidoscopic pictures. The editor stopped drinking his tea, and said, "By Jove, it's something new! Original. Refreshing." And they bought my pictures and gave them a half-page spread. Then the Beaverbrook Group, who publish the *Daily Express* and the *Sunday Express,* picked them up and syndicated them all over the world. They were used for greeting cards and for calendars. It proved my point that good pictures will sell themselves. . . .

There are photographic fanatics, just as there are religious fanatics. They buy a so-called candid camera . . . there is no such thing: it's the photographer who has to be candid, not the camera. . . .

Life is better than ever now. There are new presidents . . . kings . . . queens . . . starlets . . . public enemies . . . Hello! Hello! Who's calling? (I wish the phone would stop ringing.) This is the White House . . . this is Buckingham Palace . . . this is the Warden of Sing Sing Prison . . . this is Alcatraz. Oh, so you want pictures? Have you got an appointment? Guess I'd better pack up my typewriter (I wish it had an attachment that could spell and write English for me) and my camera and get going to . . . Paris . . . London . . . Berlin . . . Rome . . . Tokyo . . . Hong Kong . . . the world is calling, and I'm on my way . . . any mail for me? Here's my passport, dearie. Just call me Weegee.

Easter Sunday in Harlem, 1940
Gelatin-silver print, 13½″ x 10½″

Helen Levitt
American, 1918 –

Most known for her understated, elegant depictions of 1940s street life in her native New York City (photographs published in *A Way of Seeing*, 1965, with an appreciation by James Agee), Levitt shared with Agee and Walker Evans a desire for direct expression of feelings in art. Her photographs of children allow access to their games and fantasy worlds as adapted to urban circumstances. Levitt supported herself with freelance magazine work and made pioneering color photographs in New York in the late 1950s and again in the early 1970s. In a statement written for this book Levitt contends:

All I can say about the work I try to do, is that the aesthetic is in reality itself.

Untitled, New York City, 1942
Gelatin-silver print, 6¾″ x 10¼″

Berenice Abbott
American, 1898 –

While living in Paris in the 1920s Abbott assisted the artist Man Ray and made portraits of the major literary and artistic figures of the time, including the great French photographer Atget just before his death in 1927. It is largely due to her efforts that his work came to public attention. Abbott brought Atget's uninflected documentary style to bear on New York City in the 1930s. This statement comes from Abbott's 1935 proposal to the Works Progress Administration Federal Arts Project. The project was funded and published in 1939 as *Changing New York*.

To photograph New York City means to seek to catch in the sensitive and delicate photographic emulsion the spirit of the metropolis, while remaining true to its essential fact, its hurrying tempo, its congested streets, the past jostling the present. The concern is not with an architectural rendering of detail, the buildings of 1935 over-shadowing everything else, but with a synthesis which shows the skyscraper in relation to the less colossal edifices which preceded it. City vistas, waterways, highways, all means of transportation, areas where peculiarly urban aspects of human living can be observed, crowds, city squares where the trees die for lack of sun and air, narrow and dark canyons where visibility fails because there is no light, litter blowing along a waterfront slip, relics of the age of General Grant or Queen Victoria where these have survived the onward march of the steam shovel; all these things and many more comprise New York City in 1935 and it is these aspects that should be photographed.

It is important that they should be photographed today, not tomorrow; for tomorrow may see many of these exciting and important mementos of eighteenth- and nineteenth-century New York swept away to make room for new colossi. Already many an amazing and incredible building which was, or could have been, photographed five years ago has disappeared. The tempo of the metropolis is not of eternity, or even time, but of the vanishing instant. Especially then has such a record a peculiarly documentary, as well as artistic, significance. All work that can salvage from oblivion the memorials of the metropolis will have value. Something of this purpose has been carried out as the exigencies of a busy life and the physical difficulties of the undertaking have permitted, but more could be done with ample leisure to devote wholly to the project and with more systematic assistance.

Tempo of the City, Fifth Avenue and 42nd Street Manhattan, September 6, 1938
Gelatin-silver print, 8½" x 7¾"

Frederick Sommer
American (b. Italy), 1905 –

Sommer began photographing after meeting Alfred Stieglitz in 1935, turning away from his training as a landscape architect. Much of his work consists of spatially ambiguous images of southwestern American desert landscape; however, he is also known for his metaphoric, surreal still-life constructions and his troubling photographs of decomposing animals found in the desert. Sommer's work is deeply thoughtful and prevents easy reading; his fine printing technique and abstract theoretical stance have been widely influential. For this book, Sommer wrote:

Design reaches for the complimentary in aesthetic fields, the splendor of design is display of pictorial logic.

Art is perception of design structured in the perceived, memorized images are the beginning of linguistic logic.

There would be no music without structure and memory, nature and logic are incapable of iconoclasm.

Jack Rabbit, 1939
Gelatin-silver print, 7½″ x 9¼″

Edward Weston
American, 1886 – 1958

One of photography's greatest artists, Weston was acclaimed both for his ground-breaking attention to the medium's innate qualities and for his commitment to aesthetic purity. As with Paul Strand, Weston's significant work began in the early 1920s after a decade's worth of Pictorialist imagery. By the end of the 1920s, however, Weston had concluded that his task as an artist was to "render the substance and quintessence of *the thing itself*," and his obsession with clear, sharp description in images of objects (particularly vegetables), landscapes and portraits inspired the formation of Group f.64 in 1932. In his *Daybooks,* Weston wrote:

July 16, 1931: Artists (fine ones) don't copy nature, and when they do record quite literally the presentation is such as to arouse connotations quite apart from the subject matter. The camera recording nature exactly can yet be used to convey an abstract idea. Peppers are reproduced in seed catalogues, but they have no relation to my peppers.

No — nature cannot be improved upon considered physically. No use to exactly copy a butterfly — better to see it floating in summer sky: but to find a dead pelican, photograph a few inches of its wing so that white quills dart from black barbs like rays of light cutting a night sky — this is not copying nature, but using her with imaginative intent, to a definite end.

February 1, 1932: Photography as a creative expression — or what you will — must be seeing plus. Seeing alone means factual recording. Photography is not at all seeing in the sense that the eyes see. Our vision is binocular, it is in a continuous state of flux, while the camera captures but a single isolated condition of the moment. Besides, we use lenses of various focal lengths to purposely exaggerate actual seeing, we "overcome" color for the same reason. In printing we carry on our willful distortion of fact. This is all legitimate procedure: but it is not seeing literally, it is seeing with intention, with reason.

An idea just as abstract as could be conceived by sculptor or painter can be expressed through "objective" recording with the camera, because nature has everything that can possibly be imagined by the artist: and the camera, controlled by wisdom, goes beyond statistics.

Pelican, Point Lobos, 1942
Gelatin-silver print, 7½″ x 9½″

Aaron Siskind
American, 1903 –

Although his planar, abstract work from the late 1940s on is recognized as some of the greatest twentieth-century American photographic art, Siskind began his photographic career under the auspices of New York City's Photo League (1936-1951), a group of photographers whose collective mission was the advancement of socially engaged documentary work. Siskind's 1941 departure from the League symbolized a decisive shift in his work (and in mid-century American photography in general) away from the primacy of subject matter per se toward the dominance of individual vision. Siskind has had great influence as a teacher, both at the Chicago Institute of Design and the Rhode Island School of Design. In the exhibition catalog, *Aaron Siskind: Photographer,* 1965, Siskind states:

When I make a photograph I want it to be an altogether new object, complete and self-contained, whose basic condition is order — (unlike the world of events and actions whose permanent condition is change and disorder).

The business of making a photograph may be said in simple terms to consist of three elements: the objective world (whose permanent condition is change and disorder), the sheet of paper on which the picture will be realized, and the experience which brings them together. First, and emphatically, I accept the flat plane of the picture surface as the primary frame of reference of the picture. The experience itself may be described as one of total absorption in the object. But the object serves only a personal need and the requirements of the picture. Thus, rocks are sculptured forms; a section of common decorative iron-work, springing rhythmic shapes; fragments of paper sticking to a wall, a conversation piece. And these forms, totems, masks, figures, shapes, images must finally take their place in the tonal field of the picture and strictly conform to their space environment. The object has entered the picture, in a sense; it has been photographed directly. But it is often unrecognizable; for it has been removed from its usual context, disassociated from its customary neighbors and forced into new relationships.

What is the subject matter of this apparently very personal world? It has been suggested that these shapes and images are underworld characters, the inhabitants of that vast common realm of memories that have gone down below the level of conscious control. It may be they are. The degree of emotional involvement and the amount of free association with the material being photographed would point in that direction. However, I must stress that my own interest is immediate and in the picture. What I am conscious of and what I feel is the picture I am making, the relation of that picture to others I have made and, more generally, its relation to others I have experienced.

New York 1, 1947
Gelatin-silver print, 13¼″ x 10″

Albert Renger-Patzsch
German, 1897 – 1966

Renger-Patzsch and Karl Blossfeldt were the most important contributors to the German "Neue Sachlichkeit" movement of the 1920s and 1930s. This "new objectivity" was the German equivalent of the American Group f.64, and Renger-Patzsch had an influence on European photography comparable to Edward Weston's in America. He was interested in precise descriptions of machinery, flora, and architecture, and his book *The World is Beautiful* (1928) demonstrated his obsession with pure, natural forms. After World War II he concentrated his energies on landscape photography. This statement comes from "Photography and Art" in *Das Deutsche*.

There was a time when one looked over one's shoulder with an ironical smile at the photographer and when photography as a profession seemed almost invariably a target for ridicule. That time is now over. A whole number of people of cultivated taste, technical ability and well-developed formal talent have made photography into a matter of serious artistic concern.

The question of whether photography *can be regarded as art or not* has given rise to much verbal and written discussion. However, it seems pointless to me to attempt to determine the question either way. After all, one can prove everything: that it is art and that it is not, that it assumes an intermediate position, that one must extend the concept of art to take account of photography, and so on.

Basically that is a question which, for reasons of organization, might interest the editor of an encyclopedia of conversation, but it has nothing to do with the real issues. Therefore we shall refrain from any attempt at classification.

But photography *exists* and has done for nearly a hundred years now. It has acquired an immense significance for modern man, many thousands of people live from it and through it, it exerts an immense influence on wide sections of the population by means of film, it has given rise to the illustrated press, it provides true-to-life illustrations in most works of a scientific nature, in short, modern life is no longer thinkable without photography.

Zierlen, ca. 1955
Gelatin-silver print, 9″ x 6¾″

Brett Weston
American, 1911 –

Like his father Edward, Brett Weston demonstrated in his work an obsession with precise, clear photographs of natural forms, landscapes, textures and bodies. His photographs were first shown at the important "Film und Foto" exhibition in Stuttgart when Weston was 18. He was also invited to show with Group f.64 in their first exhibition in 1932. Although the impact of his images was somewhat pre-empted by the strength of his father's, the younger Weston's work indicates a greater interest in abstraction, atmosphere and graphic formalism. This statement from March 1975 was originally published in *Dialogue with Photography*.

I photograph man-made things a great deal. It's true, I am a modern man in many ways. I love modern architecture, modern machines and tools. . . .

. . . I don't limit myself. I hope I'm not too stylized or too much in a rut. I use various types of cameras and photograph anything, anytime. It could be something modern or an ancient rock, it doesn't matter. But, unless a landscape is invested with a sense of mystery, it is no better than a postcard. . . .

My whole life is photography, but I love music. I have dear friends who are musicians and writers as well as photographers. I also love traveling. . . .

When I photograph, I don't have anything in mind except the photograph. I don't think in terms of magazines, books, or promotions. I photograph for the love and the excitement. It's just a self-centered, dedicated thing. . . .

. . . a dedication to photography and freedom. That's all I want. I don't want a lot of money. Freedom is the paramount thing — the freedom to work. It's very hard in our times, with all the material abundance around us, to have it. We're distracted — we want this and we want that. . . .

I don't photograph for other people. I love an audience, mind you. Once I've got them there, then I love an audience. Not a big audience, though. I'd rather please ten people I respect than ten million I don't. But I don't play to an audience, I do it for myself.

Portugal, 1960
Gelatin-silver print, 9½″ x 7½″

Minor White
American, 1908 – 1976

White served photography as a teacher, a critic, an innovative publisher and an influential image-maker. In all of his pursuits, including *Aperture* magazine (which he founded in 1952 and edited until 1975), he sought to infuse his work with spiritual aspects of creativity and lessons derived from Oriental thought and Gestalt psychology. He felt that his photographs — fine black-and-white prints, often of natural subjects — should be viewed as metaphors for human experiences. This statement was originally published in *Minor White: Rites and Passages*.

The path my feet took was lined with images, whole gardens of pictures. With exposures I picked bouquets, each more vivid than the previous . . . finally a gathering of gem-like flames in the low tide . . . I thought I had forgotten how to use my camera, so I counted each step of the process aloud . . . shutter speed, aperture, cock the shutter. . . . Though I feared to lose the sense of beauty, no loss occurred; the sense of rapport was strong beyond belief.

While rocks were photographed, the subject of the sequence is not rocks; while symbols seem to appear, they are pointers to the significance. The meaning appears in the space between the images, in the mood they raise in the beholder. The flow of the sequence eddies in the river of his associations as he passes from picture to picture. The rocks and the photographs are only objects upon which significance is spread like sheets on the ground to dry.

Eleanor, Chicago, 1953
Gelatin-silver print, 6″ x 7½″

Wynn Bullock
American, 1902 – 1975

Bullock invoked the purist aesthetics of the western, Group f.64 tradition in his fine prints of nudes, nature scenes and buildings; however, he extended the tradition to account for his conception of photography as an abstracting medium, one that should "express the fourth-dimensional structure of the real world." Trained extensively in music, Bullock experimented with techniques for registering and reproducing light, which he considered as pervasive and pliable as sound. Some of his writings were published posthumously in *Photographing the Nude*.

The urge to create, the urge to photograph, comes in part from the deep desire to live with more integrity, to live more in peace with the world, and possibly to help others do the same. . . .

As I became aware that all things have unique spatial and temporal qualities which visually define and relate them, I began to perceive the things I was photographing not as objects but as events. Working to develop my skills of perceiving and symbolizing these event qualities, I discovered the principle of opposites. When, for example, I photographed the smooth, luminous body of a woman behind a dirty cobwebbed window, I found that the qualities of each event were enhanced and the universal forces which they manifested were more powerfully evoked. Out of these experiences, I embarked on some of my most productive years of working.

Nude Behind Cobwebbed Window, 1955
Gelatin-silver print, 9¼″ x 7¼″

W. Eugene Smith
American, 1918 – 1978

One of the most important American photojournalists, Smith conducted his work under the principle "let truth be the prejudice." His famous photo-essays ("Spanish Village," "Nurse-Midwife," "Country Doctor," Schweitzer in Africa) helped define the look of *LIFE* magazine in the 1940s and 1950s, and established a model for subsequent work in the essay form. Smith was compassionate toward his subjects and uncompromising about the use of his images, maintaining control over editing and even layout of his stories. This statement is from "The World's Greatest Photographers," in the May 1958 issue of *Popular Photography*.

I doubt the existence of any perfection, although I am for trying the rise to this the impossible and would take measure from such failure rather than from the convenience of a safe but mundane success. (I do not deplore success.) I would experience even deeper, and endeavor to give out from this experience. My photographs at best hold only a small strength, but through them I would suggest and criticize and illuminate and try to give compassionate understanding. And through the passion given into my photographs (no matter how quiet) I would call out for a spiritualization that would create strength and healing and purpose, as teacher and surgeon and entertainer, and would give comment upon man's place and preservation within the new age — a terrible and exciting age. And with passion. Passion, yes, as passion is in all great searches and is necessary to all creative endeavors — whether of statesman, or scientist, or artist, or freedom, or devil — and Don Juan may have been without passion, for sex and sentiment and violence can very much be without passion. Question this? Take note of the values around you, everywhere thrust upon you — and wade awhile, with this question in thought, through publications and publications from cover to cover.

The Thread Maker, 1951
Gelatin-silver print, 13⅜" x 9⅛"

Robert Frank
American (b. Switzerland), 1924 –

From his non-native observer's position, Frank made incisive photographs exposing the underside of 1950s American culture. His landmark book *The Americans* (published in the United States in 1959) confirmed the emergence of a new subjectivity in American photography and established Frank as one of the most important and influential small-camera photographers in the medium's history. After the publication of the book, Frank began to make films and is now widely recognized for his directorial innovation. Before the publication of *The Americans,* Frank wrote an essay for *U.S. Camera Annual 1958* discussing his approach to photography. From that essay, he selected a statement for this book.

Above all, I know that life for a photographer cannot be a matter of indifference. Opinion often consists of a kind of criticism. But criticism can come out of love. It is important to see what is invisible to others. Perhaps the look of hope or the look of sadness. Also, it is always the instantaneous reaction to oneself that produces a photograph.

Fourth of July, Jay, New York, 1955-56
Gelatin-silver print, 13⅜″ x 9″

William Klein
American, 1928 –

Though his mastery of the 35mm medium may be compared to Cartier-Bresson's, Klein was much more interested in the photographer's effect on situations than the willfully invisible Cartier-Bresson. Klein's provocative and grittily engaging "street photography" challenged traditions of elegance, discretion and formal quality. His books — *New York* (1956), *Rome* (1958), *Moscow* (1962) and *Tokyo* (1964) — resemble psychological portraits of cities more than photojournalistic documentation. Klein's work for *Vogue* (1955-1965) expanded the boundaries of fashion photography. This statement is from Klein's book *Rome*.

All roads lead to Rome, even mine, and all Romes exist, even mine. You might not have found my Rome looking for yours — but you might have also failed to find other Romes, the pretty, miserable white-color Rome, or the hopeless Rome of the unemployed, or Holy Rome, or Ancient Rome, or Café Society Rome. This book is a result of several months spent in Rome, several visits and something of several Romes, what I have seen and what I think I have seen. I might be wrong but if I am wrong, then, I am wrong. . . .

Sunday dinner at the sea-shore is quite an affair. An Italian pointed out to me that the social equivalent of these families in France would probably be picnicking on the beach. Aside from the fact that macaroni boiling is difficult in the sand, it would seem to be beneath Italian dignity to eat below table level. If you are going to take your family out for a day you can damn well sit them down in a restaurant, call a waiter and be a sport — even half naked, peeling, and sand-caked in any one of the twenty, noisy, 500-lire trattorie on the Ostia beach.

But, very important, note that the whole family, including prospective sons and daughters-in-law, is together, because they want to be, around this table. Here, exhibit A, is the secret of Italian Happiness and Equilibrium. The family in Italy is not a No Man's Land as it is elsewhere but a mutual admiration society where parents and children adore each other unself-consciously. Children are free, spoiled, and listened to. Parents are indulgent and contrary to all logic, inducible from American experience, children are well-adjusted, and — so help me — parents are respected.

Every holiday is also a family holiday where the old are as spoiled as the young. Family solidarity thus becomes a form of old-age insurance.

Ostia Beach, Rome, 1956
Gelatin-silver print, 13½″ x 9⅝″

Bruce Davidson
American, 1933 –

In numerous documentary photo-essays, on subjects including a traveling circus, a gang of Brooklyn youths, the Civil Rights movement and the New York subway system, Davidson has proved himself as a compassionate observer of the lives of common Americans. Associated with Magnum Photos since 1958, his extended projects have come to epitomize the agency's notions of personally motivated, concerned photography. Davidson published *East 100th Street,* a study of a stricken Harlem neighborhood, in 1970, and he has also directed a number of films. This statement was written for his 1978 book *Bruce Davidson Photographs.*

The man who headed the picture library at Magnum told me about a small circus that had pitched its tent at Palisades Amusement Park in New Jersey. I began to photograph the circus every day during the weeks it was there; then I traveled with it along its route. I took pictures of the circus acts — the girl riding the elephant, the lion tamer, the man shot from the cannon and the clowns. I rode with the cannon man and his family in a silver truck that carried his cannon. The roustabouts helped me climb the rim of the tent to the top, where I saw the circus far below.

I first saw the dwarf standing outside the tent in the dull mist of a cold spring evening. His distorted torso, normal-sized head and stunted legs both attracted and repelled me. He stood sad and silent, smoking a cigarette outside the tent.

Loud music played and he disappeared into the lights and laughter of the tent. His name was Jimmy, but he called himself "Little Man," and sometimes after the last show we went into a diner together where people snickered and laughed at us. When I finished the photographs of him, I gave Jimmy a small camera that could fit into his hands. . . . I finished the dwarf essay in the summer of 1959.

Jimmy Armstrong, 1958
Gelatin-silver print, 12″ x 8″

Diane Arbus
American, 1923 – 1971

For Arbus, one of the most influential American artists of the 1960s, photography was a process of confrontation. Her direct, uncompromising portrayals of individuals out of the social mainstream reveal her fascination with experience beyond her urban, upper-class, sheltered upbringing. Arbus's work refigures both traditional portraiture and the nature of documentary photography. A collection of her writings was published posthumously, in the 1972 monograph *Diane Arbus*.

If I were just curious, it would be very hard to say to someone, "I want to come to your house and have you talk to me and tell me the story of your life." I mean people are going to say, "You're crazy." Plus they're going to keep mighty guarded. But the camera is a kind of license. A lot of people, they want to be paid that much attention and that's a reasonable kind of attention to be paid. . . .

What I'm trying to describe is that it's impossible to get out of your skin into somebody else's. And that's what all this is a little bit about. That somebody else's tragedy is not the same as your own. . . .

Freaks was a thing I photographed a lot. It was one of the first things I photographed and it had a terrific kind of excitement for me. I just used to adore them. I still do adore some of them. I don't quite mean they're my best friends but they made me feel a mixture of shame and awe. There's a quality of legend about freaks. Like a person in a fairy tale who stops you and demands that you answer a riddle. Most people go through life dreading they'll have a traumatic experience. Freaks were born with their trauma. They've already passed their test in life. They're aristocrats. . . .

I never have taken a picture I've intended. They're always better or worse.

For me the subject of the picture is always more important than the picture. And more complicated. I do have a feeling for the print but I don't have a holy feeling for it. I really think what it is, is what it's about. I mean it has to be *of* something. And what it's of is always more remarkable than what it is.

I do feel I have some slight corner on something about the quality of things. I mean it's very subtle and a little embarrassing to me, but I really believe there are things which nobody would see unless I photographed them.

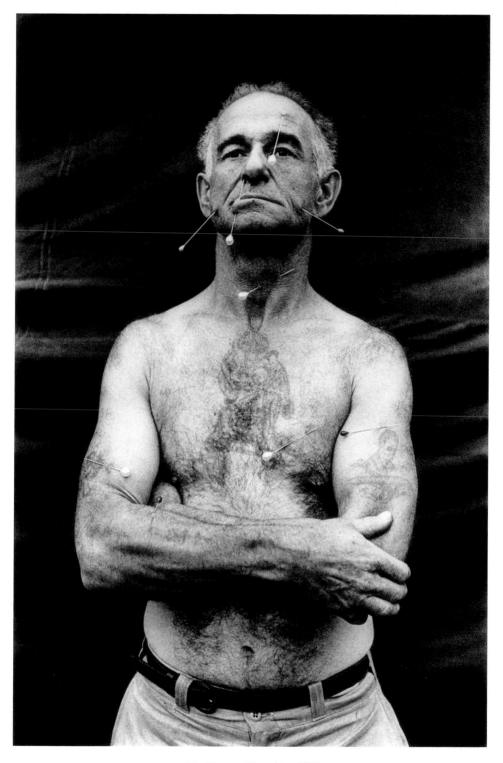

The Human Pincushion, 1962
Gelatin-silver print, 10″ x 6⅝″

Garry Winogrand
American, 1928 – 1984

Winogrand's quick and intricate observations of the social landscape, eloquent elaborations on the snapshot aesthetic, prompted Museum of Modern Art curator John Szarkowski to label him "the central photographer of his generation." Winogrand's central principle — "I photograph to find out what the world looks like photographed" — led him to make pictures at an astounding rate; when he died he left behind more than 300,000 unedited exposures. Winogrand was included in the 1967 Museum of Modern Art exhibition "New Documents" with Diane Arbus and Lee Friedlander and was again honored by the Museum of Modern Art with a large-scale postmortem retrospective in 1988. In 1974 Winogrand wrote the following essay about his work:

Understanding Still Photographs

There is nothing as mysterious as a fact clearly described. What I write here is a description of what I have come to understand about photography, from photographing and from looking at photographs.

A work of art is that thing whose form and content are organic to the tools and materials that made it. Still photography is a chemical, mechanical process. Literal description, or the illusion of literal description, is what the tools and materials of still photography do better than any other graphic medium. A still photograph is the illusion of a literal description of how a camera saw a piece of time and space. Understanding this, one can postulate the following theorem: Anything and all things are photographable.

A photograph can only look like how the camera saw what was photographed. Or, how the camera saw the piece of time and space is responsible for how the photograph looks. Therefore, a photograph can look any way. Or, there's no way a photograph has to look (beyond being an illusion of a literal description). Or, there are no external or abstract or preconceived rules of design that can apply to still photographs.

I like to think of photographing as a two-way act of respect. Respect for the medium, by letting it do what it does best, describe. And respect for the subject, by describing it as it is. A photograph must be responsible to both.

I photograph to see what things look like photographed.

Woman with Ice Cream Cone, New York City, 1968
Gelatin-silver print, 8¾″ x 13¼″

Lee Friedlander
American, 1934 –

Friedlander's photographs of cityscapes, monuments, vegetation, social events, and industrial sites reveal a highly sophisticated vision presented in a seemingly haphazard fashion. His work appeared in the important "New Documents" show at the Museum of Modern Art in 1967 (with Garry Winogrand's and Diane Arbus's), helping to define the new photographic genre of "social landscape." Friedlander was also responsible for saving and printing the work of the New Orleans photographer E.J. Bellocq in 1968. In the introduction to his 1970 monograph *Self Portrait,* he writes:

I suspect it is for one's self-interest that one looks at one's surroundings and one's self. This search is personally born and is indeed my reason and motive for making photographs. The camera is not merely a reflecting pool and the photographs are not exactly the mirror, mirror on the wall that speaks with a twisted tongue. Witness is borne and puzzles come together at the photographic moment which is very simple and complete. The mind-finger presses the release on the silly machine and it stops time and holds what its jaw can encompass and what the light will stain. That moment when the landscape speaks to the observer.

Knoxville, 1971
Gelatin-silver print, 7¼″ x 11″

Robert Adams
American, 1937 –

In both his writings on photography and his gently persuasive images of man-altered western American landscapes, Adams manifests an acute awareness of and desire for beauty in the face of change. His work, along with that of Lewis Baltz, Frank Gohlke and others was included in the important 1975 exhibition "New Topographics" at the George Eastman House, a show that explored the transformative effects of human culture on nature. In his 1974 monograph, *The New West*, Adams explained his peculiar approach to photographing the landscape.

Many have asked, pointing incredulously toward a sweep of tract homes and billboards, why picture *that*? The question sounds simple, but it implies a difficult issue — why open our eyes anywhere but in undamaged places like national parks?

One reason is, of course, that we do not live in parks, that we need to improve things at home, and that to do it we have to see the facts without blinking. We need to watch, for example, as an old woman, alone, is forced to carry her groceries in August heat over a fifty acre parking lot; then we know, safe from the comforting lies of profiteers, that we must begin again. . . .

The subject of these pictures is, in this sense, not tract homes or freeways but the source of all Form, light. The Front Range is astonishing because it is overspread with light of such richness that banality is impossible. Even subdivisions, which we hate for the obscenity of the speculator's greed, are at certain times of day transformed to a dry, cold brilliance.

Towns, many now suggest, are intrusions on sacred landscapes, and who can deny it, looking at the squalor we have laid across America? But even as we see the harm of our work and determine to correct it, we also see that nothing can, in the last analysis, intrude. Nothing permanently diminishes the affirmation of the sun.

Along Interstate 25, 1968
Gelatin-silver print, 5½" x 6"

Paul Caponigro
American, 1932 –

Caponigro's on-going love for music can be sensed in his mystical, poetic photographs of nature. He depicts both details and the wider landscape in masterful black-and-white prints. Minor White, his major influence, published many of Caponigro's photographs in *Aperture* magazine in the 1960s. Caponigro is also widely experienced as a teacher, having led courses at Yale, Princeton, Boston University and New York University. This statement is from the preface to his 1983 book *The Wise Silence*.

In my years of photography I have learned that many things can be sensed, seen, shaped, or resolved in a realm of quiet, well in advance of, or between, the actual clicking of shutters and the sloshing of films and papers in chemical solutions. I work to attain a "state of heart," a gentle space offering inspirational substance that could purify one's vision. Photography, like music, must be born in the unmanifest world of spirit.

For me, intellectual manipulations, forced combining elements in the name of design, even the best arrangements of the mind are of limited value in this realm of beauty. I strive to undo my reactions to civilization's syncopated demands and hope that inner peace, quiet, and lack of concern for specific results may enable a stance of gratitude and balance — a receptiveness that will allow the participation of grace. This meditative form of inaction has been my true realm of creative action. A dynamic and vital seeing is my aim.

I do not necessarily visualize complete images, but rather, my intent is to sense an emotional shape or grasp some inner visitation. My wish is to partake of the "hush" experienced on first glimpse of the Unicorn in the wood. The stuff of mythology and the substance of earth's atmosphere are of the intangible. The magic brought forth by such images as the Unicorn is also available in that solid place we refer to as the real world. It is my conviction that the earth and all its manifestations contain this magic. Who has not, at certain times and in certain terrain, felt the stillness of atmosphere that places a hush on the land? And who has not been affected by that unique agitation generated by the light of the full moon? Permeating the arid deserts and attending the cyclic lappings of water at the shores of seas and lakes is the pulse and breath of earth itself. Even as I have passed through museum halls lined with the efforts of artists and craftsmen from many ages, I have felt that same thrill of vital life emanate from a truly great work of art. Achieve the mystery of stillness, and you can experience a dynamic interaction with the life force that goes far beyond intellectual thought and touches the deepest wells of existence.

I would like to think that I am approximately in my middle years of working as a photographer and that I have time to continue. I am most grateful for the discovery and conviction that the real working is internal. Calm and inner stillness are for me essential companions to the activity of my craft.

Monument Valley, Utah, from *Portfolio II,* 1970
Gelatin-silver print, 6¾″ x 8½″

Josef Sudek
Czechoslovakian, 1896 – 1976

Sudek's lyrical images, simple and intimate renderings of small details and private moments, have earned him the title of "the Poet of Prague." After 1926, Sudek never traveled outside of Czechoslovakia. His work was shown in a major 1936 exhibition in Prague with that of Moholy-Nagy, Man Ray, John Heartfield and Alexander Rodchenko; in 1961 he was the first photographer honored by the Czech government as an "Artist of Merit." Two of his major bodies of work were series called *Windows* and *Magic Gardens*. This statement is from the book, *Sudek*.

I print my photographs exactly the way a graphic artist prints the engraving or the etching on his printing press. I want nothing else but that the camera with its lens delivers what I myself put in front of it. . . .

I have no particular leaning toward . . . the all-too-clearly defined; I prefer the living, the vital, and life is very different from geometry; simplified security has no place in life.

Everything around us, dead or alive, in the eyes of a crazy photographer mysteriously takes on many variations, so that a seemingly dead object comes to life through light or by its surrounding. And if the photographer has a bit of sense in his head maybe he is able to capture some of this — and I suppose that's lyricism.

When a person likes his profession and tries hard to overcome the difficulties that are connected with it, then he is glad if at least something of what he tried to do succeeds. I think that is enough for a lifetime. And while you're at it you work up a real sweat and that's a bonus. . . .

I never cease to be surprised at young people's interest in my pictures. I can only explain it in the context of a certain longing for romanticism, for good old craftsmanship. But that will pass, and in a few years their interest will lie somewhere different. But prophesies are always risky. The critics of my generation never visualized photography as an independent branch of art; today this is accepted as a matter of course.

I don't like the discussions about whether photography is an art. Even though I think that if it would be just a craft I would not have stayed with it all my life. . . .

This profession does not have a long tradition. A hundred years? What is that? A lot depends on skill. Until now it is not possible to photograph with the eyes only. When I want to accomplish something I do it all alone. That's why I don't go into color photography, that is a complicated profession that I don't know. To have one's material developed elsewhere, that would bother me. . . .

I believe a lot in instinct. One should never dull it by wanting to know everything.

One shouldn't ask too many questions but do what one does properly, never rush, and never torment oneself.

View of Trees from the Beautiful Park, 1971
Gelatin-silver print, 6¾″ x 9¼″

Emmet Gowin
American, 1941 –

Gowin's extended series of introspective, ethereal portraits of his wife and children provides an intimate yet public view of private experiences. Having studied with Harry Callahan at the Rhode Island School of Design in the mid-1960s, Gowin proceeded to employ wide-angle lenses and expressive prints to dramatically enhance straight photographic descriptions of his subjects. In addition to his black-and-white work with his family, Gowin has also explored landscape photography and color imagery with Polaroid films. This statement, written in 1983, was submitted by Gowin for this project.

Little Lamb and the Average Man

During the winter of 1980, five photographers were selected by the Seattle Arts Commission to photograph in Washington State. The whole state, we were told, was ours for a subject. My thoughts began to fill with visions of city life and rain forests, agriculture and forestry, as I waited for June and July. On May 18, 1980, Mount St. Helens erupted. Looking back, it seems to me another instance of a subject extending itself towards me. I wonder if I would have traveled to Mount St. Helens on my own. But many things beyond our control work together on our behalf; chance and choice and human action combine and contribute to the quality of our lives.

By a second chance, the head of the Photographic Section of the U.S. Forest Service, William Hauser, was waiting in the same office lobby of the Gifford Pinchot Forest the morning I explained my desire to land and photograph in the tightly guarded "Red Zone" of the still very dangerous volcano. Although he was himself a visitor in that office, a bystander, he entered our conversation. "I like your description," he said, "I'd like to help you acquire the permission you need." He then spent much of the next two days working on behalf of someone he did not know and whose aims he knew only through an impulse. Life builds when we trust our feelings; individual acts of thoughtfulness form the bonds that bring us together.

During the years 1788-94, the great English poet William Blake wrote a cycle of poems, *The Songs of Innocence*. It is fascinating to consider that these youthful poems of openness were written at a moment in England's history when the Industrial Revolution, "England's dark and satanic mills" as Blake called them, had already worked a seemingly irreversible change in the life of the average man. To such a man, nature was either something he owned and was free to exploit, or nature was a place he could seldom go, perhaps only on his vacation.

In a poem on spring, Blake wrote the deceptively simple lines, "Little Lamb, Here I Am." Rightly, in our time, we have become acutely aware of the destructive forces in nature and we do not find it possible to exclude man from our picture. "Little Lamb, Here I Am," conveys the openness with which the complex man may in some moments stand before the rigor of nature. We may even glimpse the means with which to accept ourselves. Before nature, what I see does not truly belong to anyone; I know that I cannot have it, in fact, I am not sure what I am seeing. May we, nonetheless, learn to value this Earth more.

To stand before nature is as imaginative as real and a state of mind is the limit of what we can see. Perceiving forces is a working problem in scale, and our position determines that scale. The two realities: the Little Lamb and the Average Man, suggest a condition far apart. Our survival and the poetic imagination require us to bring the two together.

Area of Mount St. Helens, 1980
Gelatin-silver print, 9¾″ x 9¾″

William Clift
American, 1944 –

Through extremely fine black-and-white printing techniques and often oversize prints, Clift depicts western American landscapes suffused with a romantic, nostalgic atmosphere that has immediate tangibility and emotional impact. He was strongly influenced by the work of Paul Caponigro, though he is primarily self-taught. Clift is also noted for his architectural photography; in 1975-1976 he was commissioned to participate in a Bicentennial documentation of American court houses. Clift wrote the following statement on November 5, 1986, for inclusion in this book.

I took this picture during a trip into Southern Colorado in 1975. That year I was very much concentrated on photographing American county courthouses for the Joseph Seagram Bicentennial Project. Thus, I was on my way along a dirt road towards a fairly small town in the mountains named Lake City, the county seat of Hinsdale County, Colorado. As was not my custom at the time, I stopped along the way and made this picture. I was struck by this view, which must have similarly impressed many others who passed before and after me. For some reason or other, this rather straightforward photograph has continued to interest me over the past ten or so years.

Trout Rising, Rio Grande, Pyramid, Colorado, 1975
Gelatin-silver print, 6¾" x 9½"

Robert Giard
American, 1939 –

Giard, a self-taught photographer educated in literature at Yale and Boston University, works primarily in the area near his Long Island home. His portraits, nude studies and landscapes are characterized by a contemplative, mysterious self-containment. Giard conveys this effect through manipulative toning of his prints and careful study of his subjects, involving preparatory sketches and historical allusions to paintings and other photographs in order to achieve an exactingly formulated result. Giard's statement was written for this book.

I choose to work with both the landscape and the portrait. Most of the landscapes are taken on the South Fork of Long Island, New York, where I make my home — a region which is at once resort, farm land, suburb, and small town. The terrain is relatively flat, and some people — painters, in particular — feel that the quality of the light is special. The landscapes that I make of this area fall roughly into two groups. There are those which are tangled and, at first glance, chaotic, like some of the Jackson Pollacks that were in fact painted here. Then there are those which are simple and austere, a bit minimalist. *Hedge and Hillock* is characteristic of the latter.

Both the specific content of the image and the form it assumes within the photograph are important considerations for me. . . . In making this type of picture, I set myself a sort of formal problem: how to achieve a strong yet subtle composition from a minimum of shapes and a tonal range of black, grays, and white within the somewhat static frame of the square. I have a liking for that stasis because it encourages a viewer to contemplate the subject itself, whether of a landscape or of a portrait. . . .

The content of a photograph is more difficult for me to talk about. For one thing, there are two kinds of content: the apparent visual content and the emotional content. I do respond to specific objects and places. This particular hedge and hil-lock happen to be part of a golf course in Southampton, the very one on which the 1986 Open was played. I am partial to golf courses; their gentle undulations and sculpted shapes furnish me with the raw materials which I seek in nature. However, this is not the sort of picture of a golf course which one is likely to encounter in the brochures. In no way is this an uninflected topographical document. It is instead a picture of a monumental and moody presence to which I am paying attention because, especially when viewed through the lens, it resonates for me. I stop short though at trying to name whatever it is that this object resonates with. In fact, my titles are utterly literal — *Circles on a Lawn, Two Hedges* — though my intentions may be less so.

Not that there isn't a genuine correlation between the Hamptons as they appear in my photographs and the Hamptons as they "really are." That starkness and that skein of vegetation are both characteristic expressions of this place, and people who spend time here year-round come to recognize as much. At the same time, I select what aspects of the landscape to photograph and record only at certain times and in certain lights. Consequently, these are highly subjective landscapes, mise en scène for a drama of silence. The face which the landscape presents to me is also the face which I turn towards the landscape.

Hedge and Hillock, 1981
Toned gelatin-silver print, 14″ x 14″

Ray K. Metzker
American, 1931 –

Metzker's photographic work in the three decades since his studies with Harry Callahan and Aaron Siskind at the Chicago Institute of Design has consisted of a series of formal visual experiments. Each series (including *Composites, Sand Creatures, Pictus Interruptus* and *City Whispers*) poses and seeks to resolve questions about the medium's descriptive potential. Though frequently abstract in appearance, Metzker's images reveal, on closer inspection, an acute, carefully defined sense of place. Originally written in his journal, this statement was published in *Unknown Territory: Photographs by Ray K. Metzker,* 1984.

For some time, I have found myself discontented with the single, fixed-frame image, the isolated moment that seemingly is the dominant concern of still photography today. Instead, my work has moved into something of the composite, of collected and related moments, employing methods of combination, repetition, and superimposition as I find the opportunity in the camera, the darkroom, and the final presentation. Where photography has been primarily a process of selection and extraction, I wish to investigate the possibilities of synthesis.

. . . I began thinking of the entire roll of film as one negative. Ten-inch sections of film were printed onto long strips of photographic paper and then mounted in rows, forming a final constructed piece which I called a composite. You can deal with the whole or you can deal with just one part. To me there is a richer experience if the two can operate together. What I am talking about is complexity. When you approach one of the large composites, you see it more as an abstract design, and when you come in closer, you see a wealth of everyday information. There is no particular point of entry or procedure to the seeing; it is a multiplicity of elements operating in an aleatory manner.

Simultaneity was a key factor — ongoing, continuous interaction of one element or form with another. My need was to integrate the variety of experience, to fashion a form that pulled diverse parts together without stripping the parts of their vitality.

At this time I was reaching into music and into flux. I was working with kinetic sculpture, building toys that would flip-flop. I didn't have the expertise for these because they needed to be electrical. So I said to myself, I know photography. Why can't I take these ideas and bring them back into photography? Percussion, the playing of one beat against the next, began to translate into the photographs.

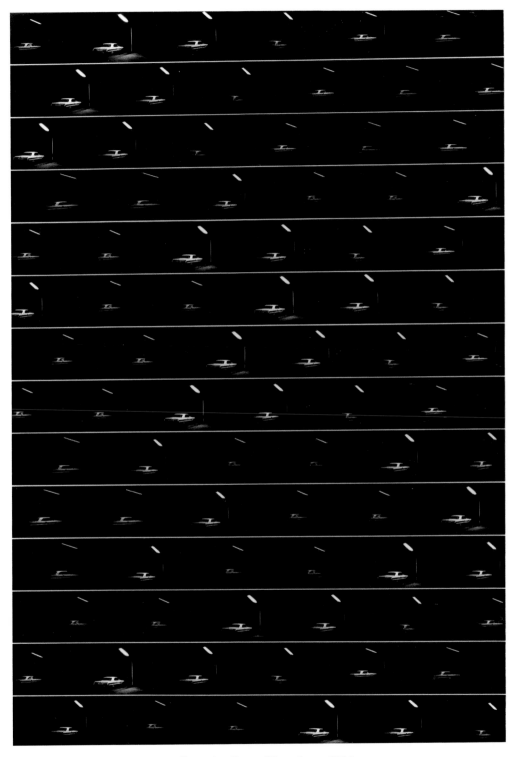

Composite: Car and Street Lamp, 1966
Gelatin-silver print, 25¼″ x 17½″

Jerry N. Uelsmann
American, 1934 –

Uelsmann's photographs are widely admired as much for their innovative technical form as for their surreal content; in fact, the seamless perfection of his combination printing creates images with an almost mythical blend of style and substance. Uelsmann's on-going concern in his work is for the relationship between natural and man-made worlds. Drawing upon the lessons of Minor White, Henry Holmes Smith and Ralph Hattersley, Uelsmann has taught photography at the University of Florida in Gainesville since 1960. Uelsmann reflects on his work for this book:

I try to begin working with no preconceived ideas. Each click of the shutter suggests an emotional and visual involvement and contains the potential of establishing greater rapport with some quintessential aspect of the subject and my feelings toward it, both conscious and preconscious. My contact sheets become a kind of visual diary of all the things I have seen and experienced with my camera. They contain the seeds from which my images grow. Before entering the darkroom, I ponder these sheets, seeking fresh and innovative juxtapositions that expand the possibilities of the initial subject matter. Ultimately, my hope is to amaze myself. The anticipation of discovering new possibilities becomes my greatest joy.

House and Daguerreotype, 1969
Montage on metal plate, 6⅜″ x 5¼″

Duane Michals
American, 1932 –

The principal concern of Michals's work is expanding the narrative capacity of photography. Drawing from Surrealism, Magritte and Zen Buddhism, Michals stages events which allow, through captions and/or sequenced images, a mixture of mundane and fantastic elements to communicate psycho-dramatic stories. His work was included (with Friedlander's, Winogrand's, Davidson's, and Danny Lyon's) in the important 1966 exhibition "Toward a Social Landscape" at the George Eastman House. Michals discussed the essence of his work for this book:

I really don't care what my father looked like, and I'm sure you don't very much either. What is important however, is what did or did not transpire between us. That lack of communication, love, conflict is my legacy, my history. This is what matters to me, and this is what I want to share with you. I write with this photograph not to tell you what you can see, rather to express what is invisible. I write to express these feelings. We are our feelings. Photography deals exquisitely with appearances, but nothing is what it appears to be.

A LETTER FROM MY FATHER

As long as I can remember, my father always said that one day he would write me a very special letter. But he never mentioned what the letter would be about. I used to try to guess what family secret the two of us would at last share, what intimacy, what mystery could now

be revealed. I know what I hoped would be in the letter. I wanted him to tell me where he had hidden his affections. But then he died, and the letter never did arrive. And I never found that place where he had hidden his love.

A Letter From My Father, 1960/75
Gelatin-silver print with text, 8″ x 10″

Robert Cumming
American, 1943 –

A highly influential teacher and visual arts theorist in the 1970s, Cumming is widely recognized for his painting and sculpture as well as his photography. His work often uses the diptych form, conveying through pairs of manipulated images a series of questions that challenge how one decodes information through photographs. Cumming often draws on facts of science, engineering and comparative analysis to validate his fictive, conceptual descriptions of photographic transformations. Cumming submitted this statement for publication in this book.

An Easterner and newcomer to Southern California in 1970, *It Was Around Dinner When The Ball Went Through The Screen* was one in a series of photo-sculptural works that began to register the unfamiliar level of illusionism in the environment. Between roughly 1973 and 1978, I produced many such pieces that resembled the vacant set photographs I'd been digging up in the movie still shops in Hollywood.

In this instance, the wood clapboard and window are a half-sized facade, a generic suburban front I'd built to function as backdrop for a number of pieces. The person and interior are a slide projection of a photo I'd taken of artist and friend Bill Wegman in Chicago five years earlier. The ball is of styrofoam and stuck on a piece of wire anchored in the window frame and the window screen is a hand-drawn grid made by scratching the large eight by ten inch negative with a needle.

It was one of a dozen similar "accident" photo tableaus woven into a broader fictional setting in 1975 in "Discourse on Domestic Disorder" (self-published, Anaheim, California).

It Was Around Dinner When the Ball Went Through the Screen, 1974
Gelatin-silver prints, 9⅝″ x 7⅝″ each

Michael Spano
American, 1949 –

Through the use of unusual equipment — wide-view and sequence-exposure cameras — and non-standard darkroom techniques, including negative solarization, Spano seeks alternative ways of representing urban experiences. His techniques expand upon the familiar genre of "street photography" to suggest the medium's potential for insight and reflection. In his portraits and nude studies he further enlarges our visual perception. Spano describes his work:

The picture reproduced here was made with a panoramic camera where the lens pans on a curved film plane while the exposure is being made, capturing 140 degrees of space at different moments on one piece of film.

A photograph representing a duration of time.

These photographs are pictures primarily of urban man. They are portraits of a people who demand a space for themselves in the territory of their experience, a domain that is both public and private. By acknowledging their territory, I establish an intimate, immediate relation with them taking the freedom to create a work of art.

Organizing a picture which depicts 140 degrees of space in the city where people are actively represented brings to bare the complex idea of grouping figures.

My figures are placed in a multi-facade deep space, with air and atmosphere around them while they move and turn. Gestures and detail are given a heightened significance pulling the composition into accord.

At the same time my awareness to the history of panoramic photography is operating. To advance the idea of this type of picture making is my challenge.

Street Scene, 1980
Gelatin-silver print, 7¼″ x 17¼″

William Wegman
American, 1943 –

Wegman's decision to name his much-documented Weimaraner "Man Ray" is an apt indication of the wit and art-historical reflexivity of Wegman's work. Like the earlier artist, Wegman fluidly switches media, creating drawings and video performance pieces as well as photographs. His imaginative and whimsical portraits of humans and canines were among the first conceptualist-influenced artworks to cross over into the largely formalist photography of the early 1970s and were included in the important 1975 exhibition "The Extended Document" at the George Eastman House. In a statement prepared for this book, Wegman says:

I liked to photograph Man Ray on the blue couch we shared from 1970 to 1982. It was also a reoccurring prop in many video pieces throughout this period. He always seemed comfortable there.

Watchful as always while working, I placed a large white museum board against him thinking I would draw or write something on it after. I liked that his fur overlapped the card breaking the illusion that its blankness was "trick photography" — but also playing with the notion.

Nothing became of this picture until after Ray died and I began to look at all the prints and negatives. The thought occurred to make a double portrait with this and another image. After trial and error, the youthful, early-70s, three-quarter portrait was selected and *Double Portrait* was made.

Double Portrait, Plate 7 from *Man Ray* portfolio, 1973/81
Gelatin-silver print, 7¼" x 7"

Irving Penn
American, 1917 –

Penn's stylized, graphically reduced fashion photographs and elegant color still-life compositions have, since the mid-1940s, defined the peak of high-style image-making. Penn has also extended his formal vision to informal subjects, treating fringe characters, cast-off objects and, most recently, skulls, with the cool distance, descriptive use of white space and exquisite prints characteristic of his work for *Vogue*. This statement was selected by Penn for inclusion in this book and is from his introduction to *Worlds In a Small Room,* 1974.

I share with many people the feeling that there is a sweetness and constancy to light that falls into a studio from the north sky that sets it beyond any other illumination. It is a light of such penetrating clarity that even a simple object lying by chance in such a light takes on an inner glow, almost a voluptuousness. This cold north light has a quality which painters have always admired, and which the early studio photographers made the fullest use of. It is this light that makes some of these early studio portraits sing with an intensity not bettered by later photographers with more sophisticated means at hand. Electric lights are a convenience but they are used, I believe, at the expense of that simple three-dimensional clarity, that *absolute existence* that a subject has standing before a camera in a north-light studio.

Mud Glove, December 1975
Platinum/palladium print, 29″ x 21″

Olivia Parker
American, 1941 –

Emerging from a background as a painter, Parker began in 1970 to use traditional photographic materials and processes (large-format negatives, toned contact prints) to convey images of found object assemblages. Through her photographs, executed in both black and white and color, Parker creates mythic frames for symbol and allusion. This statement, written in 1984, was submitted by Parker for this book.

For ten years I have been investigating the human implications of objects and the visual mental structures people have devised at various times in order to attempt an understanding of the unknown.

To explore the human implications of objects, texts, markings and other possible indicators I must find ways of changing the obvious references of subjects. My intention is not to document objects but to see them in a new context where they take on a presence dependent on the world of each photograph. Often I use old objects, for as the Polish artist Magdalena Abakanowicz said: "I am much more interested in an old piece of burlap than a new one, for the beauty of an object is to me, in the quantity of information I can get from it, the stories it has to tell." If I use new or organic materials, they only become interesting in context; a flower and a machine part must act on each other. . . .

I have mentioned my interests. My means are photographic. I do not save my constructions as permanent pieces, because their wholeness is too dependent on light and the nature of my photographic materials. By working in both black and white and color, I have a range suited to the subtleties I seek to explore. Also, although we think of photography as more "real" than the other visual arts, it allows for transformation of objects in ways I find especially interesting. The substance of an object can be altered by removing it part ways through an exposure. Light can change forms and structure. Objects or figures can exist as shadows yielding only some of their information to a piece. Color can be the color of an object as we think of it, the color of light around an object, or a new color caused by filtration, additional projected colored light, or the peculiar way a certain film and print material see color. Although my work may move close to the other visual arts in that I make what I photograph, it remains purely photographic in its final form.

Bosc, 1977
Selenium-toned gelatin-silver print, 4¾" x 6⅝"

Jan Groover
American, 1943 –

In her on-going exploration of photography's formal conventions and limitations Groover, who worked in painting and drawing during the 1960s, has utilized numerous techniques and experimented with a variety of subjects. Her work in the early 1970s involved color triptychs of architectural details and urban scenes; subsequently she made color images of intricate kitchen utensil still-lifes, platinum prints of cityscapes, close-up portraits and table-top arrangements of found objects. In each project, Groover seeks to ascertain the ideal balance between style and substance in the print. This statement is taken from an interview by Carolyn Carr, originally published in Akron Art Institute's *Dialogue,* 1979.

I was fortunate to have the understanding of the silverware business when I did. It's such wonderful stuff. It reflects everything all the time. It's so liquid in terms of its ability to pick things up. It's so transformable; a knife can be a knife and a color too. It can be a silver knife next to a silver bowl, and another knife next to it can be pink. I like that kind of visual switch.

How do I get the different colors? I have a very funny lowered ceiling right over my still-life table. Generally to get enough light on the still life you have to bounce light off all kinds of things. You can't use direct light because direct light on the silverware makes an ugly glare. . . . I found you can position certain colored cloths, or plants, or whatever out there so that you can make the color in them reflect on one thing and not another, or on all things except one by having different tilts and angles of reflection. I bounce the light off the color and position the color exactly where I want it to hit on a reflected surface. It's using them like mirrors. . . .

The activity of looking at a photograph is that you are looking at something; it's like looking at a tree or looking at a painting. I care about how something looks and I make pictures that show that care in some way or another.

I think one of the things that has irritated me about photography is the intellectual lack of wanting to talk about pictures as pictures instead of all this talk about subject matter. I think a lot of photographers are pictorially illiterate. . . . When people ask about a painting they don't necessarily say it is about a house; yet, in photography, that is the general usage and I don't like that because it is so limited. . . .

One of the hardest things in life and art is to know what you want. It seems to me that the business of making art is to push toward — I always feel weak saying it, although I know it is the truth when I think about it — is that you are always pushing to find out what you want out of a situation, and it is not anything knowable until you know it.

You can't have a game plan except in working. Photography is a fluid activity; it's not a football game.

Untitled, 1978
Type C print, 14¾″ x 18¾″

Robert F. Heinecken
American, 1931 –

An influential educator regarding the use and theory of mixed materials, Heinecken demonstrates in his collage works an interest in media commentary and, often, in the consideration of explicit sexuality. He describes his works as being not "pictures of" something, but "objects about" a theme, combining elements of sculpture, drawing and print-making to elaborate on the basic photographic message. In the early 1960s, Heinecken was responsible for introducing photography studies into the University of California at Los Angeles art department. Heinecken explains his work for this book.

Woman Contemplating Red was one of the first of six or seven pieces made over a one-year period using the same materials and basic premise. Most of the subsequent pieces utilized the underlying magazine collage in a more fractured and asymmetric way than this example and with a more specific topical cultural event (Vietnam, etc.). In *Woman Contemplating Red* the figure image in the film overlay tends to create an "accurate" silhouette rather than mixing with a conflicting magazine collage silhouette.

The four more-or-less horizontal bands correspond approximately to identifiable sections/parts of the figure and were selected to be read to represent clothing, anatomy, viscera or skin or, hopefully, combinations of these. My own exact motives for subject choices of the collage material are now rather vague — however, they are clearly symbols connoting fine, smooth texture (hair); pliable, glistening, sensual (raw meat, I think); hot, smoldering (charcoal coals); and clean, slippery, tactile (soap suds). As I write this, I realize that all are highly tactile and/or touch conscious. I also suspect that each surface could be used in any section with similar results — but, of course, different subjective associations would form.

The title was ideated after the piece was completed and is based on the downward gaze of the model, which I took to represent more simply over-rational or self-awareness and, of course, the dominant color of reds. During this period I typically used titles which lead the viewer into a rather literary interpretation or association.

One final note — the negative used to make the film overlay was purchased from a mail-order catalog outfit in Los Angeles which provided images on undeveloped film (to keep the operation legal) by description but are unseen until developed by the purchaser. In this instance, the description *might* have been: #627 World War II type pin-up poses, frontal nudity, full figure, head looking down, Caucasian, Candy McLaughlin, one 120 roll, black and white, 12 different exposures, $6.00 This idea intrigued me because the figurative image is just another "found object" in the spirit of Dada like the magazine collage material. It is authentic and societal rather than subjective and personal, and of course it was less complicated than getting a friend and cheaper than hiring a professional model.

Woman Contemplating Red, 1966
Unique print (black and white film transparency over magazine collage), 17⅞″ x 13″

David Hockney
English, 1937 –

Working first with Polaroid images, then with borderless 35mm prints, Hockney created between 1981 and 1983 hundreds of photographic collages. Internationally recognized as a painter, he first made photographs as sketches for his work. Although frustrated by the visual limitations of the single image, he realized that joining many photographs together could provide a multi-perspective redefinition of a place and incorporate elements of time and spatial manipulation absent from straight photography. In a November 1983 lecture at the Victoria and Albert Museum, Hockney elucidated his approach to photography.

Cubism was about the destruction of a fixed way of looking. A fixed position implies we are standing still, that even the eye is still. Yet we all know our eyes move constantly, and the only time they stop moving is when we're dead — or when we're staring. And if we're staring, we're not really looking. That is the problem with the single frame photograph: all you can actually do is stare at it. Your eyes cannot wander around in it, because of its inherent lack of time. When I realized that my new conception of photography was related to cubism, I made two deliberate pastiches of a cubist still life — I set up a guitar, tobacco can, wooden table, and so on — all the elements of a cubist still life. I thought the result told you far more about the presence of objects in the world than one single picture would. . . .

It made me look at cubism in another way: I saw new worlds of perception, still unexplored. It dawned on me that what we call realist painting has not [been] able to deal with cubism. It always tends to go back to the one point perspective idea, or into a kind of fluid fantasy that was nonetheless based on one point perspective. But to deal with the reality of what's around us has been a very hard thing for painters, outside of Picasso, Braque or Gris. There's not that much been done. The originators of cubism had done great things with it. And I disagree with the belief that Picasso abandoned cubism; I believe he was a cubist painter all his life. Of course, the modern idea is that cubism leads to abstraction. It appears to, and does in one sense, but cubism wasn't about abstraction, it was about the visible world, the world around us.

Cubism tends to deal with things very close to us. The closer we get to anything the more the view shifts. Cézanne pointed this out — that as the thing got closer he had more and more doubts, I discovered in photography that as things get closer to you, it gets more and more difficult to see, more and more difficult to piece together. It made me believe that the most interesting and mystical space we have is here, close to us, and not in outer space.

Almost all cubist pictures are about things close to us. They don't jump off the wall at you. *You* have to go to *them*, and look, and look. The camera does not bring anything close to you; it's only more of the same void that we see. This is also true of television, and the movies. Between you and the screen there's a window, you're simply looking through a window. Cubism is a much more involved form of vision. It's a better way of depicting reality, and I think it's a truer way. It's harder for us to see because it seems to contradict what we believe to be true. People complain that when they see a portrait by Picasso where, for instance, somebody has three eyes, they say: But people don't have three eyes! It's much simpler than that. It's not that the person had three eyes, it's that one of the eyes was seen twice. This reads the same way in my photographs. The fact that people *can* read photographs in this way made me think we've been deceived by the single photograph — by this image of one split second, in one fixed spot. I now see this fault in all photographs, and I can tell when drawings or paintings have been made from photographs. You can sense when the picture is not felt through space.

David Graves, Looking at Bayswater London, November 1982
Ektacolor print collage, 42½″ x 25½″

Cindy Sherman
American, 1954 –

Sherman's work to date consists largely of thematically focused groups of imagined, carefully staged environmental portraits in which the artist herself acts as subject. Revealing close attention to details of lighting, mise en scène, make-up, costuming and pose, the images put forth an extended thesis about cultural stereotypes, role-playing, mythical narratives and photographic representation. Her work, done mostly in the last decade, has been exhibited internationally and has garnered tremendous critical and public acclaim. This statement is from the *Documenta 7* exhibition catalog, 1982.

I want that choked-up feeling in your throat which maybe comes from despair or teary-eyed sentimentality: conveying intangible emotions.

A photograph should transcend itself, the image its medium, in order to have its own presence.

These are pictures of emotions personified, entirely of themselves with their own presence — not of me. The issue of the identity of the model is no more interesting that the possible symbolism of any other detail.

When I prepare each character I have to consider what I'm working against; that people are going to look under the make-up and wigs for that common denominator, the recognizable. I'm trying to make other people recognize something of themselves rather than me.

I have this enormous fear of being mis-interpreted, of people thinking the photos are about me, that I'm really vain and narcissistic. Then sometimes I wonder how it is I'm fooling so many people. I'm doing one of the most stupid things in the world which I can't even explain, dressing up like a child and posing in front of a camera trying to make beautiful pictures. And people seem to fall for it. (My instincts tell me it must not be very challenging then.)

Believing in one's own art becomes harder and harder when the public response grows fonder.

Untitled, 1983
Type C print, 34½″ x 20½″

Lucas Samaras
American (b. Greece), 1936 –

Since first using Polaroid materials in 1969, Samaras has expanded the descriptive ability of the instant photography medium. Through controlled colored lighting, lengthy exposures, manipulating the emulsion during its development process and cutting and reassembling prints, Samaras invests with artistic value materials generally employed for snapshot imagery. His descriptions of light and movement reflect an aesthetic that could only be realized in photography. This statement is from an interview by John Gruen, originally published in *ARTnews,* April 1976.

I have found for myself an uncultivated field to which I can go and do my stuff. That uncultivated field is the self. Most of us have evaded the body. There is a certain word which has negative connotations: narcissism. You know . . . Don't look in the mirror! Well, when you live alone, you don't have people saying "Don't do this" and "Don't do that." You can do whatever the hell you like, and if you want to look in the mirror, it's not all that dangerous, and not even all that erotic. For me, looking in the mirror produces a sense of wonder. I say, "Who is that?" I look at my hand or at my rear-end and say, "What is that?" The idea of the mirror being an area of erotic conflict is an idea for those who *don't* look into mirrors.

And so, I started photographing myself, and found that I could see portions of myself that I had never seen before. Since I face just my face in the mirror, I know pretty much what it's like. When I see a side-view, I'm not used to it, and find it peculiar. Or the back of my head — it's very strange to see it. So, photographing myself and discovering unknown territories of my surface self, causes an interesting psychological confrontation. You face certain facts about yourself. Although we all live in fantasies, and we all know that we will die some day, we have to come to terms with other unknown facts about us. At any rate, when I began photographing myself, I could place myself in poses that had not been investigated by other artists. It was an area other artists hadn't touched. Then, I went on from there. I manipulated my image — distorting it, brutalizing it. People thought I was mad, but I felt I had to tell these things. It gave me a kind of excitement. . . .

But an artist must have an involvement with everything that is in front of him, whether it's a woman, a man, a cup, a dog, a string or a tree. If an artist does not have an erotic involvement with everything that he sees, he may as well give up. To be a human being may be a very messy thing, but to be an artist is something else entirely, because art is religion, art is sex, art is society. Art is everything.

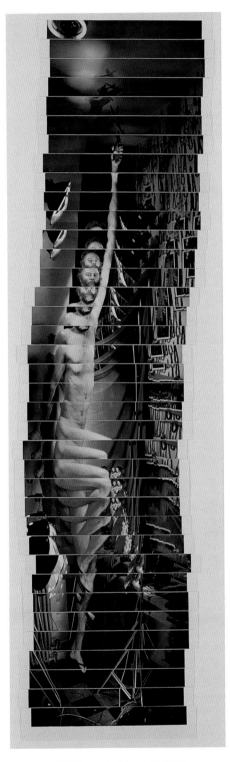

Self Portrait, March 2, 1983
Polacolor II assemblage, 33⅞″ x 9″

Bibliography

Abbott, Berenice. *Changing New York*. New York: Dutton, 1939.

Adams, Ansel. *Ansel Adams: An Autobiography*. Boston: Little, Brown and Company, 1985.

Adams, Robert. *The New West*. Boulder: Colorado Associated University Press, 1974.

Arbus, Diane. *Diane Arbus*. Edited by Doon Arbus and Marvin Israel. New York: Aperture, Inc., 1972.

Atkins, Anna. *Sun Gardens: Victorian Photograms by Anna Atkins*. New York: Aperture, Inc., 1985.

Baudelaire, Charles. "The Salon of 1859," *Art in Paris 1845 – 1862*. Translated and edited by Jonathan Mayne. Oxford: Phaidon Press Ltd., 1981.

Brandt, Bill. *Camera in London*. London: The Focal Press, 1948.

Brassaï. *Picasso and Company*. New York: Doubleday, 1966.

———. *The Secret Paris of The 30's*. Translated by Richard Miller. New York: Random House, Inc., 1976.

Bullaty, Sonja. *Sudek*. New York: Clarkson N. Potter, 1978.

Bullock, Wynn. *Photographing The Nude*. Edited by Barbara Bullock-Wilson and Edna Bullock. Salt Lake City: Gibbs M. Smith, Inc., 1984.

Callahan, Harry. *Harry Callahan: Eleanor and Barbara*. New York: The Checkerboard Foundation, 1983. Film.

Caponigro, Paul. *The Wise Silence: Photographs by Paul Caponigro*. Boston: Little, Brown and Company, 1985.

Carr, Carolyn. "Jan Groover Photographs: An Interview." *Dialogue*, Akron Art Institute, September, 1979.

Cartier-Bresson, Henri. *The Decisive Moment*. New York: Simon and Schuster, 1952.

Coburn, Alvin Langdon. "The Relation of Time to Art." *Camera Work*, Number 36, 1911.

Cunningham, Imogen. "Portraits, Ideas, and Design." Interview with Edna Tartaul Daniel, 1961. Regional Cultural History Project, Bancroft Library, University of California, Berkeley.

Davidson, Bruce. *Bruce Davidson Photographs*. New York: Agrinde Publications Ltd., 1978.

Documenta 7. Exhibition catalog. Kassel: P. Dierichs, 1982.

Emerson, Peter Henry. *Naturalistic Photography for Students of the Art*. London: Sampson Low, Marston, Searle and Rivington Limited, 1889. Reprint. New York: Arno Press, 1973.

Evans, Frederick. *The Photographic Journal* 59 (April 30, 1900):236-41.

Fenton, Roger. *Roger Fenton Photographer of The Crimean War: His Photographs and His Letters from The Crimea*. New York: Arno Press, 1973.

Flaubert, Gustave. *Flaubert in Egypt: A Sensibility on Tour*. Translated and edited by Francis Steegmuller. Boston: Little, Brown and Company, 1972.

Frank, Robert. *U.S. Camera Annual 1958*. New York: U.S. Camera Publishing Corp., 1957.

Friedlander, Lee. *Self Portrait*. New York: Haywire Press, 1970.

Gernsheim, Helmut. *Lewis Carroll: Photographer*. New York: Chanticleer Press Inc., 1949.

Gilpin, Laura. "The Fine Art of Photography." *Ninety-Eight-Six*, (May 24, 1928):7.

Gruen, John. "The Apocalyptic Disguises of Lucas Samaras." *ARTnews*, Vol. 75, No. 4, April 1976.

Hill, Paul, and Thomas Cooper. *Dialogue with Photography*. New York: Farrar, Straus and Giroux, Inc., 1979.

Hine, Lewis. "Social Photography, How the Camera May Help in the Social Uplift." *Proceedings, National Conference of Charities and Corrections* (June 1909).

Hockney, David. *David Hockney on Photography: Lecture at the Victoria and Albert Museum.* New York: André Emmerich Gallery, 1983.

Jackson, William Henry. *Time Exposure: The Autobiography of William Henry Jackson.* New York: Van Rees Press, 1940. Reprint. Albuquerque: University of New Mexico Press, 1986.

Katz, Leslie. "An Interview with Walker Evans." *Art in America,* March-April, 1971.

Kertész, André. Interview with Brooks Johnson, New York, May 11, 1982.

Kline, William. *Rome: The City and Its People.* New York: Viking Penguin, Inc., 1960.

Laughlin, Clarence John. *Clarence John Laughlin: The Personal Eye.* New York: Aperture, Inc., 1973.

Leroy, Jean. *Atget: magicien du Vieux Paris.* Translated by Jefferson C. Harrison. Joinville Le Pont: Pierre-Jean Balbo, 1975.

Mellor, David, ed. *Germany: The New Photography 1927-1933.* London: Arts Council of Great Britian, 1978.

Moholy-Nagy, László. "From Pigment to Light." *Telehor,* Vol. 1, No. 2, 1936.

Muybridge, Eadweard. *Animals in Motion.* Edited by Lewis S. Brown. New York: Dover Publications, Inc., 1957.

————. *Animal Locomotion.* Philadelphia, J.B. Lippincott, 1887.

Newhall, Beaumont, ed. *Photography: Essays and Images.* New York: Museum of Modern Art, 1980.

Penn, Irving. *Worlds in a Small Room.* New York: Grossman, 1974.

Peppiatt, Michael. "Balthus, Klossowski, Bellmer: Three Approaches to the Flesh." *Art International,* Vol. 17, No. 8, October 1973.

Ray, Man. *Man Ray Photographs.* Paris: Philippe Sers, 1981. New York: Thames and Hudson Inc., 1982.

Renger-Patzsch, Albert. "Photographie und Kunst." *Das Deutsche Lichtbild,* 1929.

Sander, August. *August Sander: Photographs of an Epoch 1904-1959.* New York: Aperture, Inc., 1980.

Siskind, Aaron. *Aaron Siskind: Photographer.* Edited by Nathan Lyons. Rochester, New York: The George Eastman House, 1965.

Smith, W. Eugene "The World's 10 Greatest Photographers." *Popular Photography,* Vol. 42, No. 5, May 1958.

Stevenson, Sara. *David Octavius Hill and Robert Adamson: Catalogue of Their Calotypes Taken Between 1843 and 1847 in the Collection of The Scottish National Portrait Gallery.* Edinburgh: National Galleries of Scotland, 1981.

Stieglitz, Alfred. Exhibition catalog. New York: Anderson Galleries, 1921.

Strand, Paul. "Photography." *Seven Arts* (Aug. 1917):524-26.

Talbot, William Henry Fox. *The Pencil of Nature.* London: Longman, Brown, Green and Longmans, 1844. Reprint. New York: Da Capo Press, 1969.

Tucker, Anne Wilkes. *Unknown Territory: Photographs by Ray K. Metzker.* New York: Aperture, 1984.

Watkins, Carleton E. Watkins Letters. Bancroft Library, University of California, Berkeley.

Weegee. *Weegee by Weegee: An Autobiography.* New York: Ziff-Davis Publishing Company, 1961.

Weston, Edward. Daybooks. Center for Creative Photography, University of Arizona, Tuscon.

————. *My Camera on Point Lobos.* Edited by Virginia Adams. Boston: Houghton Mifflin Company, 1950.

White, Minor. *Minor White: Rites and Passages.* New York: Aperture, Inc., 1978.

Index

Abbott, Berenice, 66

Adams, Ansel, 36

Adams, Robert, 100

Adamson, Robert, 8

Arbus, Diane, 94

Atget, Eugène, 26

Atkins, Anna, 10

Bellmer, Hans, 54

Brandt, Bill, 60

Brassaï, 58

Bullock, Wynn, 84

Callahan, Harry, 82

Caponigro, Paul, 102

Carroll, Lewis, 22

Cartier-Bresson, Henri, 52

Clift, William, 108

Coburn, Alvin Langdon, 32

Cumming, Robert, 118

Cunningham, Imogen, 38

Davidson, Bruce, 92

DuCamp, Maxime, 14

Emerson, Peter Henry, 24

Evans, Frederick, 28

Evans, Walker, 48

Fenton, Roger, 12

Frank, Robert, 88

Friedlander, Lee, 98

Giard, Robert, 110

Gilpin, Laura, 46

Gowin, Emmet, 106

Groover, Jan, 128

Heinecken, Robert F., 130

Hill, David Octavius, 8

Hine, Lewis Wickes, 34

Hockney, David, 132

Jackson, William Henry, 16

Kertész, André, 42

Klein, William, 90

Laughlin, Clarence John, 80

Levitt, Helen, 64

Metzker, Ray K., 112

Michals, Duane, 116

Moholy-Nagy, László, 44

Muybridge, Eadweard, 20

Parker, Olivia, 126

Penn, Irving, 124

Ray, Man, 50

Renger-Patzsch, Albert, 74

Samaras, Lucas, 136

Sander, August, 56

Sherman, Cindy, 134

Siskind, Aaron, 72

Smith, W. Eugene, 86

Sommer, Frederick, 68

Spano, Michael, 120

Stieglitz, Alfred, 30

Strand, Paul, 40

Sudek, Josef, 104

Talbot, William Henry Fox, 6

Uelsmann, Jerry N., 114

Watkins, Carleton E., 18

Weegee, 62

Wegman, William, 122

Weston, Brett, 76

Weston, Edward, 70

White, Minor, 78

Winogrand, Garry, 96